THE STAINED GLASS OF ST. PAUL'S

Beautiful Windows into Bible Mystery and Chattanooga History

Researched and written by
Jasper A. Reynolds, Jr., and Jasper A. Reynolds III
Chattanooga, Tennessee

2023

IngramSpark | La Vergne, Tennessee

Copyright © 2023, Jasper A. Reynolds III

All rights reserved. This book or any portion thereof may not be reproduced or used in any manner whatsoever without the express written permission of the author except for the use of brief quotations in a book review.

Windows photographic images courtesy of Ed Barels.
Used by permission.

Historical photographic portraits taken from one volume of eight scrapbooks compiled by E. Y. Chapin, Walter Cline, and Frank F. Stoops of the Chattanooga Half-Century Club. Courtesy of Chattanooga Public Library's Digital Collection. Used by permission of the Chattanooga Half-Century Club.

Scripture citations, except where noted, follow the numeration of the Revised Standard Version of the Bible (in accordance with the *Book of Common Prayer),* copyright © 1946, 1952, and 1971 the Division of Christian Education of the National Council of the Churches of Christ in the United States of America.
Used by permission. All rights reserved.

Printed in the United States of America

First Printing, 2023

ISBN 2370000641120

www.StPaulsWindows.com

CONTENTS

What Makes These Windows Special 5

Walking Tour Map 8-9

1. Key-Andrews Hall Vestibule

    Patten Light of the World Window: "*Is There a God?*" 10

2. Strang Chapter Room

    Record Window: "*Aren't All Religions Essentially the Same?*" 16

3. Clerestory (Epistle Side)

    Chapman Window: "*Is There Hope Beyond the Grave?*" 22

    Reeves Windows: "*Does God Still Speak to Us Today?*" 28

    Rathburn Window: "*Who Is Jesus, and Why Did He Come?*" .. 34

4. Clerestory (Gospel Side)

    Alexander Parable Windows: "*Will the World Come to an End?*" 40

5. St. George's Chapel

    Staley Window: "*Would a Loving God Allow Suffering and Evil?*" 50

    Garvin St. George Window: "*How Generous Does God Expect Me to Be?*" 56

continued on next page

6. Nave

Davidson-Brown Window: "*Why Can't We All Get Along?*" 62

7. Apse

Nieland-Overmyer Musical Angels Windows: "*Do Angels Watch over Us?*" 68

8. Apse Corridor

Ellis Window: "*Why Wouldn't Jesus Save Himself?*" 74

Nelson Window: "*Why Are Some of Jesus' Teachings So Hard to Accept?*" 80

Lasley Window: "*Was Jesus God or Man?*" 84

Ray Window: "*How Did We Get Here, and Why Do We Suffer?*" 90

Noll Window: "*Why Do Bad Things Happen to Good People?*" 96

9. Nave

Andrews Window: "*What Must I Do to Know God?*" 102

10. Key-Andrews Hall Vestibule

Kidd Baptismal Window: "*Why Observe Baptism?*" 108

Hailey Eucharist Window: "*Why Celebrate Communion?*" ... 112

Bibliography 117

WHAT MAKES THESE WINDOWS SPECIAL

Remembering St. Paul Episcopal Church in the 1970s and 1980s, I would often admire the beautiful stained glass windows as the congregation gathered for worship. While I occasionally would recognize a Bible scene or two, their larger story remained shrouded in mystery, and I wondered what these elaborate pictures were saying. As for the vaguely familiar names inscribed in the windows, my father would share stories about these long-departed Chattanooga citizens whose names lived on in stained glass.

After his death in 2000, I discovered a box containing drafts, photographs and sketches—the beginnings of a book on the stained glass at St. Paul's. Brief teasers appeared in the parish cookbook, *Cooking up Memories*. At the urging of my mother, Nilza M. Reynolds, I agreed to a seemingly impossible task which has evolved into a labor of love: completing his book. So, with a *Book of Common Prayer* and Bible in one hand and microfilm viewer in the other, I set out to discover the stories and faces behind each window.

I never dreamt these windows would teach me so much about the Christian faith or the amazing hometown cherished by so many of us. I have not found a finer collection of historic stained glass in all Chattanooga. These beautiful windows that I (and possibly others) had admired on Sundays are not only beaming with color, but they're also steeped in biblical symbolism and saturated with local history. That's not all. Just when I thought the writing was complete, I pulled back and was amazed by a new discovery: Far from an accidental collection of individual masterpieces, these windows collectively tell a much larger story addressing some of our deepest questions about life and death, joy and suffering, God and humanity. I had stumbled upon a "pearl of great price."

In the following pages, my father and I hope to acquaint you with the great stories, great people and great truths behind each window. While some windows highlight a single scene, others unfold entire dramas from the Bible or Chattanooga history. Color photographs appear throughout the book, thanks to Ed Barels. Let me suggest gazing at the windows in person, examining each one *in the order presented here*. Claim a pew in quiet discovery or sit with a friend. Ask God for eyes to see the larger story behind the pictures, not simply admire the artistry, beautiful as it is.

I am grateful to old friends who have labored before me to dedicate, create and preserve these windows: Elizabeth Bryan Patten, Herbert Kaiser, Kinchen Exum and Joe Duncan, to name a few. Without their foundational work, none of my window dressing would have been possible. May God bless you in reading my father's book as richly as God has blessed me in completing it.

J.A.R. III
Chattanooga, Tennessee
2023

Remembering the St. Paul's Stained Glass Window Committee from the 1970s and 1980s that worked tirelessly to preserve and expand St. Paul's collection, left to right: Elizabeth Bryan Patten (1907-1990), Herbert W. Kaiser, Jr. (1918-1989), Kinchen W. Exum (1922-1994) and Joseph C. Duncan (1920-2010).

The Stained Glass of St. Paul's

WALKING TOUR MAP

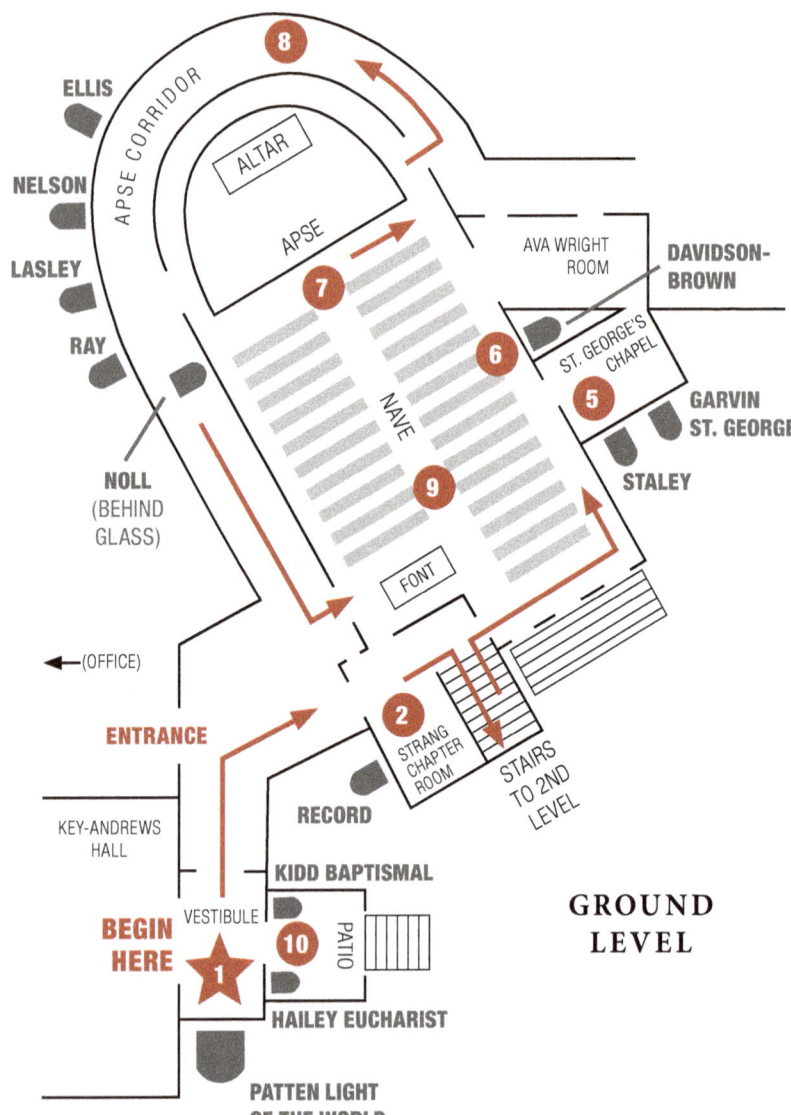

GROUND LEVEL

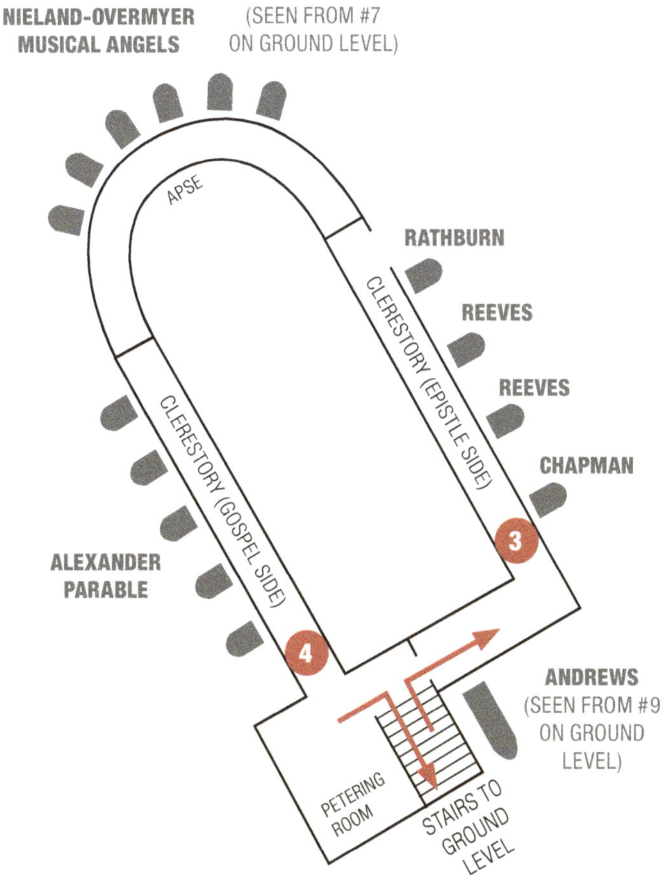

The Stained Glass of St. Paul's

NIELAND-OVERMYER MUSICAL ANGELS (SEEN FROM #7 ON GROUND LEVEL)

APSE

CLERESTORY (GOSPEL SIDE)

CLERESTORY (EPISTLE SIDE)

RATHBURN

REEVES

REEVES

CHAPMAN

ALEXANDER PARABLE

③

④

ANDREWS (SEEN FROM #9 ON GROUND LEVEL)

PETERING ROOM

STAIRS TO GROUND LEVEL

SECOND LEVEL

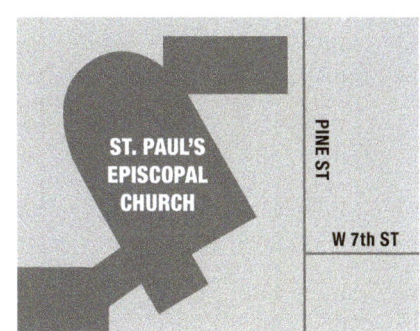

ST. PAUL'S EPISCOPAL CHURCH

PINE ST

W 7th ST

305 West 7th St., Chattanooga, Tennessee

Design: Chapel Studios, London, 1981

1. Key-Andrews Hall Vestibule

Patten Light of the World Window

Is There a God?

From time immemorial men and women have wrestled with God's existence. We look around and see death, suffering, poverty and injustice. Is there a God? God knew, in his infinite wisdom, that his creatures would have such lingering doubts, so he left us with several "lights" that testify, "There is a God, and I am He!" The Patten Light of the World window in the Key-Andrews Hall vestibule depicts these three "lights" with vivid grandeur.

The window is in memory of Sarah Key Patten (1864-1958), Mrs. Z.C. Patten, a lifelong communicant of St. Paul's. Given by the Z. Carter Patten, Jr., family, it was dedicated on Thanksgiving Day, 1981. Made by London's Chapel Studios, it is a colorful tapestry of brown, orange, yellow, green and red. In the artist's own words, "Overall there is a strong vertical accent to the design, as for a Gothic shape this is a fairly squat opening which needs such an emphasis. The group of vertical lines at the top of the window suggests the Gothic canopies found in most traditional windows, without actually being defined as such." Notice also how these vertical lines, accentuated in yellow and brightest in the center, point upward to the God they are meant to illuminate.

The Story in the Window

The first light that God gave us that we may know he exists is his beautiful creation:

> *And God said, "Let there be lights in the firmament of the heavens to separate the day from the night; and let them be for signs and for seasons and for days and years, and let them be lights in the firmament of the heavens to give light upon the earth." And it was so. ... Ever since the creation of the world his invisible nature, namely, his eternal power and deity, has been clearly perceived in the things that have been made.[1]*

From the tiniest atom to the largest galaxy, God's beautiful and complex creation clearly evidences his existence. The hymnist writes that the earth, sea and sky all proclaim the Lord's power and presence—"whose might they show, whose praise they tell."[2] We see the light of creation depicted on the right-hand side of the Patten window with scenes from our city's magnificent natural landscape. The Tennessee River winds through the familiar mountains, ridges and landmarks. At the top are Lookout Mountain and Raccoon Mountain. Halfway down on the right is Walden's Ridge, and below it the lake formed by Chickamauga Dam. Near the bottom are Maclellan Island, Moccasin Bend and Williams Island. For decades the Patten family has worked to preserve the beauty of Chattanooga's natural and historic landscape.

Another light that God gave us is the good works done by his people. Jesus said,

> *You are the light of the world. Let your light so shine before men, that they may see your good works and give glory to your Father who is in heaven.[3]*

We often think of "good works" as volunteering at a homeless shelter or supporting the arts. But good works also include the way we treat others, our words and even our inmost thoughts. The greatest good work of all is to nourish and multiply the family of God. We see this depicted on the left-hand side of the window, where the artist has documented the growth of the Episcopal Church in Chattanooga. At the bottom is Old St. Paul's, once at the northwest corner of

---

1 Genesis 1:14, 15; Romans 1:20.
2 "The Word Whom Earth and Sea and Sky" 1982 Hymnal, no. 263.
3 Matthew 5:14-16.

Chestnut and Eighth streets, illuminated by the blazing cannon fire of Chattanooga's military occupation during the War Between the States. Built in 1858-61, the building was seized temporarily as a U.S. hospital and warehouse. Issuing forth are those daughter parishes or missions that we have sponsored in the community, starting from the bottom: Grace in Brainerd (1887), Thankful Memorial in St. Elmo (1898), Christ on McCallie Avenue (1900), In as Much Mission in Rossville (1920), Mission Chapel of St. Mary the Virgin on East Eighth Street (1924), Good Shepherd on Lookout Mountain (1928), St. Timothy's on Signal Mountain (1955), St. Peter's in the Dupont community (1958) and the Church of the Nativity in Fort Oglethorpe (1966). As we survey this impressive record, we might be tempted to assume we've done enough. Yet the world is full of suffering and injustice, and so the light of our good works must burn on. Lest we think too highly of ourselves and our accomplishments, we dare not forget that "we are his workmanship, created in Christ Jesus for good works, which God prepared beforehand, that we should walk in them."[4] God deserves all the credit, even for "our" good works.

Finally, the brightest light that God gave us that we might never doubt his existence is his Son:

> *As long as I am in the world, I am the light of the world ... He who has seen me has seen the Father.*[5]

This window beautifully captures Christ in a long, white robe. His arms are outstretched over creation to his right and our good works on the left, as if to signify himself as the one "great light"[6] that outshines all others. Jesus came to illuminate what God expects of his people: perfect love for one another and complete submission to our Father's perfect will. Jesus is the brightest picture we have of who God is and what God is like. "God is light and in him is no darkness at all." And it is God's will that his people "may shine with the radiance of Christ's glory."[7]

---

4 Ephesians 2:10.
5 John 9:5; 14:9.
6 Matthew 4:16.
7 Book of Common Prayer, 215.

It is ironic to note that historic attempts to snuff out these "lights" have only intensified their glow—highlighting God's existence even more. For example, persecution of the church often has resulted in a proliferation of Christian good works. Entire forests wiped out by wildfires naturally reseed themselves within a few years. And the unjustly crucified Messiah rose again from the dead, proving he is God and ushering in the forgiveness of sins for all who believe.

The Story of the Family

Sarah Key Patten was the matriarch of a Chattanooga family of forward-thinking pioneers, entrepreneurs and conservationists. Known throughout the South for her gracious hospitality, for 50 years she welcomed public and private social occasions to Ashland, the colonial revival home built by her husband in Chattanooga Valley in 1905-06. A charter member of the Chattanooga Audubon Society, she possessed a deep love and knowledge of flowers, and she supplied blooms for various occasions and organizations. She was born Sarah Avery Key on August 16, 1864, in Fort Defiance, N.C., where her parents had taken refuge during the War Between the States. Her mother was Elizabeth Jane Lenoir, born in Ross' Landing, which would become Chattanooga. Her father was Judge David McKendree Key, who after serving under Confederate Gen. Caswell, returned with his family to practice law in this city. He became a U.S. senator, postmaster general and judge. Miss Sarah Key was in Japan visiting her brother, Commodore Albert Lenoir Key, when she received a letter from Zeboim Cartter Patten proposing marriage. She and the 62-year-old widower were united on January 28, 1902. She died on July 18, 1958, and is buried at Forest Hills Cemetery, St. Elmo.

Z.C. Patten was one of the Chattanooga's most influential civic leaders and a key contributor to the city's early commercial growth. He organized or owned five companies that remained prominent a century later. Born in Wilna, N.Y., on May 8, 1840, to John Adams Patten and the former Betsy E. Cartter, he fought in the 115th Illinois infantry regiment, was wounded at the Battle of Chickamauga in 1863 and first saw Chattanooga while convalescing in the makeshift hospital at "Old St. Paul's". Mr.

Patten returned here after the war, where he opened a newsstand, book and stationery store later known as T.H. Payne & Co. Mr. Patten briefly owned *The Chattanooga Daily Times*, forerunner of today's *Times Free Press*. His greatest commercial legacy was organizing the Chattanooga Medicine Co. (Chattem) in 1879, from which he made his fortune. In his 60s, Mr. Patten established Volunteer State Life Insurance Co. and Stone Fort Land Co. This latter firm oversaw the commercial development of 11th and Market Streets, now the site of Warehouse Row, sparking the greatest economic development in Chattanooga history. In 1907-08 he financed the construction of the Patten Hotel to rival the Read House. Patten Parkway was named in his honor in 1944. His first wife, Mary Miller Rawlings Patten, died, leaving him to raise a daughter who would marry Coca-Cola bottling pioneer John Thomas Lupton. Mr. Patten died on March 20, 1925, and is buried at Forest Hills Cemetery.

Z. Cartter Patten, Jr. continued his family's tradition of business success and public service, particularly in nature conservancy. His parents' only child, he was born on February 2, 1903. Like his parents before him, he raised his own family at Ashland. He served in the Tennessee state Senate and House of Representatives, the Hamilton County Council and the 1964 state constitutional convention. He served in several of his father's businesses, most notably as an officer at Volunteer State. He was devoted to local history, authoring several books, and to local conservation, for which he received many honors as a leader in forest management. He died on February 5, 1982, and is buried at Forest Hills Cemetery.

Elizabeth Nelson Bryan Patten shared her husband's passion and leadership in historical preservation and natural conservation. She was a leading advocate of the Tennessee River Gorge, and a key force in restoring Fort Wood, the Victorian neighborhood just east of downtown where many of Chattanooga's early families lived. At St. Paul's, Mrs. Patten served on the vestry, Altar Guild and Stained Glass Window Committee. She also served as chairman of the 125th parish anniversary celebration and honorary chairman of the building centennial in 1988. She was born on October 1, 1907, in Nashville to Dr. Worcester Allen Bryan and Emma Horatia Berry Bryan. She and Mr. Patten were married on August 31, 1931, and had four children: Sarah Patten Gwynn, Emma Berry Patten Casey, Z. Cartter Patten III and W.A. Bryan Patten. She died on February 8,1990, at Memorial Hospital, which she had helped to found 40 years earlier, and is buried at Forest Hills Cemetery.

The Stained Glass of St. Paul's

Design: Chapel Studios, London, 1983

2. Strang Chapter Room

Record Window

Aren't All Religions Essentially the Same?

Imagine 10 blind men trying to identify an elephant. One feels for the trunk, another embraces a leg, still another grabs an ear, while another is poked by the tusk. Though each one reports a different experience, aren't they all handling the same elephant? So it is often said of religion. With so many doctrines and deities dotting human history, couldn't we assume they're all diverse expressions of the same thing?

Not so, says St. Paul, who encountered this very mindset in ancient Athens. So afraid were the Athenian Greeks of offending an overlooked deity that they built scores of temples to all kinds of gods, sacrificing to each one. But in trying to cover all their bases, they made a terrible error: treating all gods the same, like flavors in an ice cream shop.

The Record-St. Paul window in the Strang Chapter Room reminds us that there is something unique about our God that sets him apart from his many contenders and pretenders. Paul recognized this as he strolled through Athens and marveled at its beautiful temples: While other religions offer mankind creative ways to pursue or please the god of each one's preference, the Christian Bible stands alone in saying we can never reach God, no matter how hard or how sincerely we try. With our Lord, it's the other way around: He pursues us.[1]

---

1 Romans 3:11; John 15:16.

The Record-St. Paul window was given by Dr. and Mrs. W.D.L. Record, he a distinguished surgeon and she the daughter of a pioneering industrialist, one of four windows charting the life of the Apostle Paul. It was designed by Chapel Studios of London and dedicated on Whitsunday, May 22, 1983, along with four other windows located elsewhere in the church. Because this window receives little direct sunlight and would have been overshadowed by the Noll window (which once occupied the adjacent wall before it was moved to its present location in the apse corridor), more restrained and lighter colors were deliberately selected. These include red, blue, green, orange and gray.

The Story in the Window

The two upper quadrants form a single scene from Acts 17:16-34. In it we observe St. Paul preaching to the Athenians on Mars Hill. As he walked around the city, he was distressed to see that Athens was full of pagan idols. Two such temples are depicted at the top of the right-hand light: the Parthenon (honoring Athena) and the Erechtheion (dedicated to multiple deities), both on the Acropolis, the ancient hill on which they still stand. Day after day Paul had reasoned in the Jewish synagogues and the public marketplace with anyone who would listen, imploring them to forsake their lifeless idols of stone and turn to the one true living God. He finally caught the notice of the Athenian intellectuals, who, worried that they had failed to include Paul's god in their city's assortment of temples, brought him to address the entire assembly.

> *So Paul, standing in the middle of the Areopagus, said: "Men of Athens, I perceive that in every way you are very religious. For as I passed along, and observed the objects of your worship, I found also an altar with this inscription, 'To an unknown god.' What therefore you worship as unknown, this I proclaim to you. The God who made the world and everything in it, being Lord of heaven and earth, does not live in shrines made by man, nor is he served by human hands, as though he needed anything, since he himself gives to all men life and breath and everything ... The times of ignorance God overlooked, but now he commands all men everywhere to*

> *repent, because he has fixed a day on which he will judge the world in righteousness by a man whom he has appointed, and of this he has given assurance to all men by raising him from the dead.*[2]

Notice the inscription "to the unknown god" in the very center of the window. The Bible's God was "unknown" to the Athenians, as he is to many in our own day, because he is unique among the many gods in human history. The god of one of the world's most prominent religions requires his adherents to prove themselves through prayers and good works; by contrast, the Bible's God accepts us "just as I am," as the familiar hymn reminds us.[3] The gods of several other religions are found in every animal, plant and rock, whereas the Bible's one God is the Creator of these things who spoke them into existence. In one very prominent religion today, followers aspire to become gods themselves, whereas the Bible's God stooped down to become one of us. In each case, can both religious expressions logically be true at once? Supposing not, how then could these all be essentially the same religion?

The Bible's God is unique from other religious expressions in yet another way: he has personally intervened in human history. In the bottom left-hand scene we see St. Paul healing the cripple at Lystra in Acts 14:8. This is an illustration of how the Bible's God brought his kingdom of love and mercy into human space and time in a tangible way. What other god has intervened so personally in human history? Because many religions view time as cyclical, historical events therefore are regarded with less meaning; in the Bible all time is counting down to a specific Day when Christ will return to redeem his people and judge the world, and therefore history has meaning.

In the bottom right-hand scene, we see a quite different picture: a storm-tossed vessel. Here is the galley in which Paul was shipwrecked on his final journey to Rome, taken from Acts 27:27-44. The ship—with its sails, masts and rigging—serves as an ancient symbol for Christ's church, pilgrims sailing through dangerous waters to reach

---

2 Acts 17:22-31.
3 "Just As I Am, Without One Plea," *1982 Hymnal*, no. 693.

their ultimate destination. For Christians, we have an ultimate destination, an actual physical place which Jesus called Paradise. St. Ambrose compared the church to a ship, with the cross as its mast, as seen in the Davidson-Brown window in the nave. The Lord used an ark to preserve Noah and his family during the Flood, and a fishing boat to carry his disciples through the tempest (Mark 4:37-41). But in each case, the Lord arose to calm the storm, leaving his people awestruck at his power and strengthened in their faith.

How many of us, like this wooden vessel, have been battered and soaked by the raging storms of life, yet have seen God's "grace and mercy speedily help and deliver us"?[4] When the church is seated together in the nave (Latin for "ship"), it is as though we are all fellow travelers on a ship—like the disciples as they sailed through the storm that Jesus calmed. While nearly every other religious expression promises rewards to those who can achieve a level of goodness or perform the right acts of obedience, not so with the Bible's God: "In this life you will have trouble," Jesus assured his followers! Elsewhere he said, "For you always have the poor with you."[5] "Count it all joy, my brethren, when you meet various trials …"[6] No other religion promises such heartache and turmoil – not exactly the best way to attract followers, is it? But those who trust in God during the storms of this life will arrive at their final destination. For like any loving parent, the Bible's God is more interested in shaping our character for eternity than insulating our peace and tranquility in this temporal life.

The Story of the Family

Dr. W.D.L. Record was a prominent Chattanooga surgeon and former chief of staff of Erlanger Medical Center. He and his wife were long-time communicants of St Paul's. He was born in Lynchburg, Tenn., the youngest of nine children of W.D.L. Record, a prominent attorney, and Sue Dance Record, who served as Moore County registrar and secretary of the Tennessee Legislature. Dr. Record studied at Morgan Prep School in Petersburg, Tenn., Vanderbilt University and Vanderbilt Medical School. He served his internship

---

[4] *Book of Common Prayer*, 212.

[5] Matthew 26:11.

[6] James 1:2.

at Nashville General Hospital and at the famed Cleveland Clinic in Ohio. A veteran of both World Wars, he attained the rank of major with the 56th Hospital Station in New Guinea in the latter war. He was a member of the Tennessee and Hamilton County Medical societies, American Medical Association, and International College of Surgeons.

Margaret Milne Record, his wife, was a Chattanooga native, daughter of Walter Scott and Mary Butland Milne. Her father was president of Milne Chair Co., a huge factory complex which he built in 1912 in the Avondale section of East Chattanooga, near Orchard Knob. Milne Street is still found there today. When the new plant opened in 1913, young Margaret was given the privilege of switching on the power. Guests were given chair spindles as souvenirs. The company ceased operation in 1950.

The Records had no children and lived in an elegant home on Minnekahda, the hill where John A. Patten had planned to develop his Riverview estate in the early 20th century; only the carriage house ever was built, which are condos to this day. They died within weeks of one another—she on September 30, 1983, and he on November 11—shortly after their window at St. Paul's was installed.

Design: Artist unknown, 1900

3. Clerestory (Epistle Side)

Chapman Window

Is There Hope Beyond the Grave?

Death is the scariest reality each one of us will ever face. When confronted by danger, sickness or life-threatening circumstances, who among us doesn't fight to stay alive? Because we are created with the inherent desire to live, we all wonder what awaits us on the other side. Have you ever found yourself asking, in your most solitary moments, if there is hope? The Julia Bloomfield Chapman window sheds light on the hope we have for life beyond the grave.

Situated on the Epistle (east) side of the nave clerestory closest to the front door of the church, this window was the gift of the Altar Guild of St. Agnes in February 1900. It is in memory of one of the guild's earliest and most devoted members and its first president. Beautiful reds and greens of flowers and vines combine with the prominent white Tudor roses to make an effective example of Art Nouveau stained glass. Regrettably, like many of our older windows, the designer is unknown.

The Story in the Window

Even though God is immortal, he takes human death very seriously. "Not wishing that any should perish," He pleads with us to "choose life, that you and your descendants may live, loving the Lord your God, obeying his voice, and cleaving to him."[1] But not only is God concerned for the life of our physical bodies. When he created us, he also gave our bodies everlasting souls. So to *choose life* means

---

1 II Peter 3:9; Deuteronomy 30:19.

choosing the salvation of our bodies and souls. Jesus taught that only the Lord "can destroy both soul and body in hell."[2] The problem is that by our very nature, all people have made a different choice: distancing ourselves from God. The consequence, as St. Paul explains in Romans 6:23, is the death of our bodies and also our souls.

Were the story to end there, we would have no hope! But God in his mercy sent us his Son to die in our place, through the great suffering of his physical death, and the greater agony of his spiritual death.[3] And while each of us must leave this world in death, Jesus' resurrection ensures that we, too, will live again on the Day he returns! As St. Paul says in that same passage, "the free gift of God is eternal life in Christ Jesus our Lord."

And this is the Chapman window's message to us. Predominant in the background is a scarlet cross and plinth, or base, almost in the form of an Easter cross. These serve as reminders that Jesus' blood was shed on a cross so that we might be presented to the Father washed of our sins "white as snow".[4] Just as vines and roses (symbols of life) have grown up to overtake the cross (ancient symbol of death, as an electric chair today), Jesus' grisly sufferings have been eclipsed by His amazing resurrection.

The white Tudor roses represent many things, including purity and virginity, two biblical virtues highly esteemed in public a century ago when the window was designed. The vines are a direct reference to Christ, "the true vine," whose true followers are "the branches".[5] Jesus used the vine and branches to illustrate the relationship between God and His people, reminding us that we derive our existence, sustenance and fruitfulness from Him. "[A]part from me you can do nothing" of lasting value; so will it be with the branches that are pruned from the vine. But we who have been grafted into the Vine (as the result of our salvation) are empowered to "bear much fruit." That is, we are to live every aspect of our lives, whether in private or before others, in

---

2 Matthew 10:28.
3 Matthew 27:50.
4 Isaiah 1:18.
5 John 15:1-8.

such a way that pleases our heavenly Father. Ultimately, the fruit we bear will show whether we really have been grafted into the Vine, or whether we have been pruned from it. The vine and branches further remind us that because our very lives belong to God, it is futile for us to pursue our own desires apart from His own.

At the top of the window is a stylized inverted onion with a gold crown. The onion, a hallmark of Orthodox church architecture, is said to represent the cosmic unity between heaven and earth in the worship of God. In other words, though we are separated by time and space from our departed loved ones and the angels and the saints of ages past, yet in Christ the two congregations are suddenly and mystically united for the purpose of worship. Jesus said, "For where two or three are gathered in my name, there am I in the midst of them."[6] The fourth stanza of hymn 525 in our 1982 Hymnal, *The Church's One Foundation*, says it another way: "Yet she on earth hath union with God the Three in One, And mystic sweet communion with those whose rest is won." It is amazing to consider that the God of the universe is not just figuratively present when we invoke His Name on Sunday mornings, but that He is literally in our midst, living inside the bodies and souls of His people. While the church has not yet achieved institutional unity on earth, we nevertheless already enjoy a spiritual unity that is unique to Christianity among the world religions.

The inscription wrapped around the golden door posts in the bottom panel is a taken from Jesus' words in Revelation 14:13: "Blessed are the dead which die in the Lord ... their works do follow them." This is one of the opening verses said in our Burial of the Dead to comfort those who mourn.[7] It is interesting to note here that our works *follow* us; they do not precede us. That is to say, the good things we may do in this present life do not win for us peace in the next life. Rather, eternal rest is a gift from God, freely given in spite of our best attempts to win His favor. It is Jesus who won God's favor for us by offering Himself on the cross in our place.

---

6   Matthew 18:25.
7   *Book of Common Prayer*, 469.

The golden doorposts are more difficult to explain with absolute certainty. Jesus referred to himself as the door or gate to the Father: "Strive to enter by the narrow door; for many, I tell you, will seek to enter and will not be able."[8] Elsewhere, "Not every one who says to me, 'Lord, Lord,' shall enter the kingdom of heaven, but he who does the will of my Father who is in heaven."[9] But in the Chapman window, the doors here likely represent the very gates of heaven. It is an understatement to say that Christ's people will weep for joy at the sight of these gates, the final destination of all those who will spend eternity with Him. In the last chapter of the Bible, Jesus says, "Blessed are they that do his commandments, that they may have the right to the tree of life, and may enter in through the gates into the city [i.e. heaven]."[10] But seeing here how the gates are closed, it is equally possible that they represent Miss Chapman's tomb, which is sealed for now but will be unsealed at Christ's glorious return: the Day when every person will be resurrected, whether for eternal judgment or eternal rest.

Encircling the memorial inscription at the very bottom are laurel leaves, representing victory or triumph for the believer, particularly over temptation and trial[11]. It was customary in ancient times to so crown the victor, whether in an athletic contest or in war. Because its leaves never wilt, the laurel also symbolizes the eternality of this crown: From the moment it is given to us, it will never be taken away.[12]

The Story of the Family

Julia Bloomfield Chapman was born in 1855 to Mrs. and Mrs. George Monizette (Mary Frances) Chapman. Originally from Brooklyn, N.Y., the family migrated to Selma, Ala., eventually settling in Chattanooga in the 1870s. Her father worked in the railroad industry. Miss Chapman, along with her sister Josephine, was instrumental in obtaining a new organ for St. Paul's in 1881.

---

8   Luke 13:24.
9   Matthew 7:21.
10 Revelation 22:14, KJV.
11 II Timothy 2:1.
12 I Peter 5:4.

She also served as a charter member of the Altar Guild of St. Agnes. Miss Chapman taught for many years in the Chattanooga public schools and was a teacher at Fairmount College for women (now DuBose Conference Center, Monteagle) when she died of pneumonia on February 15, 1900, in Baltimore. Her body was returned to Chattanooga, for burial at Forest Hills Cemetery, St. Elmo, in the presence of many friends, including members of the Chattanooga Music Club, of which she had been vice president. There were many flowers including an arrangement specially designed by the Music Club. Dr. Charles A. Garratt presided at the organ she helped to obtain and played the funeral marches of Beethoven, Chopin and Handel, and a double quartet chanted a psalm and sang two favorite hymns. Josephine, her sister, survived her until 1911.

Design: Artist unknown, 1896

3. Clerestory (Epistle Side)

REEVES WINDOWS

Does God Still Speak to Us Today?

In the beginning God talked to Adam and Eve face to face as a friend, walking with them in the Garden of Eden. But when our first parents blatantly violated his command and his trust, open communication between God and mankind all but ceased. God did not reject his people entirely as throughout the Old Testament we see God reaching out to them through dreams, visions, angels and other means. In the New Testament he spoke to us through his Son.[1] And as two windows in the nave clerestory remind us, God still speaks to us today, through his written Word and through answered prayer, especially in the midst of life's trials and sorrows.

On the Epistle (east) side of the clerestory are two windows dedicated in 1896 by Frances M. Starrett Reeves: the first in memory of her husband, Dr. James Edmond Reeves (1829-96), "Beloved Physician;" the second as a future memorial to herself. Unlike the others, these two windows are of a cloudy glass. They contain slightly muted tones of brown, blue and green predominantly, as well as red, yellow and white. The lower panels of both windows are ostensibly of different tonal quality. It is believed that the upper panels may have come from Old St. Paul's, at the corner of Eighth and Chestnut streets, before they were dedicated as memorials in the present building. The lower ventilators containing the memorial inscriptions were added later to accommodate the new building's taller architecture. The extensions are of rippled glass. In 1924, parts of the windows were damaged by vandals and later repaired with purple slag glass.

---

1 Hebrews 1:1-2.

The Story in the Window

It was once thought that these windows depicted St. Joseph, the Virgin Mary and the boy Jesus. But, as we shall see, their subjects are actually other well-known saints in the Bible who share uncanny similarities with Dr. and Mrs. Reeves.

Dr. Reeves' window, closest to the high altar, depicts St. Luke, a fellow physician and writer. Christian artists traditionally depict Luke holding a book and quill, as he does here. Luke accompanied St. Paul on some of his missionary journeys across the Roman world, recording the life, death and resurrection of Christ from surviving witnesses and documenting the early Church's explosive growth. His writings today are known as the Gospel according to Luke and the Acts of the Apostles. Both of these New Testament books were written to Theophilus, who may have been a Greek new believer or a Gentile seeking to learn about the life and influence of Christ:

> *In asmuch as many have undertaken to compile a narrative of the things which have been accomplished among us, just as they were delivered to us by those who from the beginning were eyewitnesses and ministers of the word, it seemed good to me also, having followed all things closely for some time past, to write an orderly account for you, most excellent Theophilus, that you may know the truth concerning the things of which you have been informed.*[2]

In places, Luke endured persecution with Paul from those who ridiculed the idea of a God suffering for his people[3], those who sneered at the possibility of an afterlife[4], and those who denied that Jesus was the only way to God[5]. Luke was with Paul in prison at the last. St. Luke is remembered every October 18 in the church calendar, and a special collect is said in gratitude to God for his life.[6]

---

2 Luke 1:1-4.
3 Acts 17:1-9.
4 Acts 17:32.
5 Acts 18:13.
6 *Book of Common Prayer*, 193.

Mrs. Reeves' window is of Hannah and her son Samuel. Because Mrs. Reeves had no children of her own, she may have identified closely with Hannah, one of the greatest women of the Old Testament, who trusted God for a son when it appeared that she would never conceive. Hannah's trials are recorded in I Samuel 1: For many years she had suffered stigma in the community and abuse from a rival wife because she had borne no children to her husband. Hannah cried out to God, vowing to consecrate her firstborn to lifelong service to the Lord, if only he would grant her a son. In his great compassion, the Lord opened her womb! Once the boy Samuel had been weaned, his determined mother handed him over to Eli the high priest, as she had vowed. "Samuel was ministering before the Lord, a boy girded with a linen ephod. And his mother used to make for him a little robe and take it to him each year, when she went up with her husband to offer the yearly sacrifice" (II Samuel 2:18-19). Notice the small purple garment in her hand. Hannah's beautiful song of celebration is immortalized in I Samuel 2:1-10. It was Samuel who, years later, would anoint Israel's first two kings, Saul and David.

Near the top of each window are large yellow and white irises. Over the centuries these three-petaled flowers have come to represent many things, including the biblical virtues of faith, wisdom and valor. The iris also points to one of the greatest mysteries of the Christian faith: the Holy Trinity. While there is only one God, he has revealed himself as three separate and distinct persons (Father, Son and Holy Spirit), all of whom share a single substance. The familiar hymn by Reginald Heber exclaims, "Holy, Holy, Holy! Merciful and mighty, God in three persons, blessed trinity!"[7]

At the apex of each window is a small medallion. The one over St. Luke contains a red flower with four petals, called a quatrefoil, commonly found in the arch of stained glass windows during the Gothic Revival and Renaissance to represent the four evangelists—in our case St. Luke. Over Hannah and Samuel is a golden crown; while the crown is symbolic of the royal authority of Jesus Christ, the King of Kings, it also represents the "crown of righteousness," or the eternal

---

[7] "Holy, Holy, Holy! Lord God Almighty" *1982 Hymnal,* no. 362.

reward that God has promised to those who love Him and continue to obey Him during hard times[8].

Both St. Paul and the prophet Isaiah taught that our human acts of righteousness "are like a polluted garment" in God's sight when compared to Christ's perfect record of righteousness.[9] For this reason, eternal rewards from God are meant not to compensate us for good behavior but, rather, to encourage us lest we despair during difficult times.[10] In fact, Jesus warned his followers that we inevitably would share in his suffering,[11] whether poverty, loneliness, childlessness or death. But for those who suffer because of obedience, God comforts them with the assurance that their work for his sake will not go unrewarded. Fittingly, the fourth thanksgiving prayer in our liturgy, titled *For the Saints and Faithful Departed*, reminds us of the eternal reward awaiting "Samuel with Hannah his mother" for their faithful obedience.[12] Every true follower of Christ will share in this reward!

The Story of the Family

Dr. James Edmond Reeves was born in Annisville, Va., on April 5, 1829, to the Rev. Josiah Washington and Nancy Mosee (Kemper) Reeves. A poor boy, he was obligated to assist his father, who was a tailor, and therefore his early education was neglected. Later after working two jobs at a time, he was able to afford Hampden Sydney Medical College and the University of Pennsylvania. He became an eminent physician, widely respected throughout the United States as an authority on microscopic science technique. For much of his career he practiced medicine in Virginia and West Virginia, writing many medical papers, serving as a public health officer and receiving numerous distinctions. He spent the latter years of his career in Chattanooga, assisting the State Board of Health in its defenses against yellow fever among other pursuits. He loved and wrote widely about Chattanooga, promoting this city to his friends around the country. He died of liver cancer on January 4, 1896, at his residence at

---

8 II Timothy 4:5-8.
9 Isaiah 64:6.
10 Galatians 6:9.
11 Matthew 10:21-25.
12 *Book of Common Prayer*, 838.

the corner of McCallie Avenue and Houston Street. *The Sunday Times* devoted nearly an entire page to his obituary. "The beloved physician passed to his reward as peacefully and quietly as though he was falling into a refreshing slumber," the paper stated. "Dr. Reeves was held in the highest esteem by all and was greatly loved and admired by a large circle of friends." He had instructed the autopsy surgeon in exactly how to proceed—his liver to be bottled intact in alcohol and sent to Dr. Osler, his friend and diagnostician at Johns Hopkins University, Baltimore, with the rest to be investigated thoroughly. The account of his final illness and the deathbed scene are scrupulously preserved in the newspaper, including the fact that his widow was prostrate at his death and could not accompany his body to its interment in Wheeling, W.Va. Dr. P.D. Sims, who had attended so many people in Chattanooga's 1878 yellow fever epidemic, accompanied the body instead. Survivors were a son and two daughters from his first marriage in 1851, none of them Chattanoogans. He had been married a second time in 1863 with no children. His obituary further noted, "He has known his condition from the first and has been quietly and patiently awaiting death with the calmness and fortitude of the Christian philosopher and has given a most eminent example of what the consolations of religion, a mind at peace with the whole world and a conscience void of offense, do for one in the hour and article of death."

Frances M. Starrett Reeves, his widow, became Dr. Reeves' third wife in 1872. She was known for her works of benevolence, particularly the Old Ladies' Home and St. Paul's, where she placed the two Reeves windows. She lived in Chattanooga until her death on May 5, 1908, and also was buried in Wheeling, W.Va. Her only survivors were two brothers in Ohio.

The Stained Glass of St. Paul's

Design: Artist unknown, ca. 1872-1888

3. Clerestory (Epistle Side)

Rathburn Window

Who Is Jesus, and Why Did He Come?

The oldest stained glass window in the church—and possibly in all Chattanooga—is a memorial to Miss Nellie Rathburn, who died at age 16 in 1872, given by her parents, Mr. and Mrs. William Perry Rathburn. Originally it stood above the altar in "Old St. Paul's," the 1853 brick building at Chestnut and Eighth streets, where the Mountain City Club now stands. Reinstalled in the present building in 1888, it is in the clerestory on the Epistle (east) side of the nave nearest to the organ pipes. This window gently uses the tragic occasion of young Nellie's death to explain who Jesus is and why he came to earth as he did 2,000 years ago.

It is extremely ornate and of high-quality glass, possibly Bohemian, and its three-pointed gothic arched panels contain both colored (stained) and painted glass. This strikingly beautiful mid-Victorian window has lovely, vibrant colors, predominantly red—to draw attention to Jesus' atoning blood shed on behalf of his people—as well as deep blue, symbolic of the heaven that awaits his people. It also contains green, yellow, purple, olive, brown, gray and white.

The Story in the Window

The focal point of this magnificent and complex window is the scene in the center panel, showing the Savior welcoming young Nellie into heaven with arms outstretched. This is a time of consolation in which Jesus will wipe away every tear. While the identity of the two women in the outer panels is unclear, the red and golden nimbi (halos) suggest that they are distinguished saints rejoicing at Nellie's arrival. The right panel is thought to be the Virgin Mary. From her emerges an anchor, the ancient symbol for Christ, who is the Anchor of men's souls amid the sure storms that will rock us in this life[1]. The woman in the left panel is more difficult to identify. Judging from her more decorative royal attire, the heavy cross in her hand, and the large stones at her feet, possibly she is St. Helena, mother of Roman Emperor Constantine. This woman oversaw the excavation of Calvary in the fourth century in search of the true cross. Could her inclusion in the Rathburn window reflect their shared English heritage, or even young Nellie's scholarly interests?

Fortunately, the rest of the window is soaked in imagery so clear that little else is left to conjecture. Each image proclaims Jesus' identity. Along the bottom row, the baptismal font declares that Jesus is the Living Water, who washes away our sins to make us clean in the Father's presence[2]. Beside it, the *Agnus Dei* ("Lamb of God" in Latin) bearing the Banner of Victory reminds us that Jesus was "like a lamb that is led to the slaughter"[3] to secure victory over death and suffering for his people[4]. It was John the Baptist who first publicly recognized who Jesus was: "Behold, the Lamb of God, who takes away the sin of the world!"[5]; no longer must God's people have to make toilsome, daily atonement for their sins by bringing animal sacrifices to the Temple. Jesus would offer his own life as the final, permanent sacrifice for all who believed[6]. Next to the *Agnus Dei*, the open Bible with sword denotes that Jesus is the sword of the Spirit, or the word of the living God[7]: "For the word of God is living and active, sharper than any two-edged sword, piercing to the division of soul and spirit, of joints and marrow, and discerning the thoughts and intentions of the heart."[8]

During times of grief, men and women have always looked to favorite Scripture verses for consolation and assurance. So it is interesting to ponder the three inscriptions selected by Mr. and Mrs. Rathburn for their daughter's window. The first is Jesus' beatitude from Matthew 5:8, inscribed inside two opposing red medallions midway up the outer

---

1 Hebrews 6:17-20.
2 John 4:10; I Corinthians 6:9-11.
3 Isaiah 53:7.
4 I Corinthians 15:54-56.
5 John 1:29.
6 Hebrews 10:1-18.
7 Ephesians 6:17.
8 Hebrews 4:12.

panels: "Blessed are the pure in heart ... for they shall see GOD" (in the old King James Version commonly used in that day). This verse from the Sermon on the Mount would have shocked Jesus' ancient audience since many in Israel, including the Pharisees, believed that a life of good deeds was earning them God's favor, or that poverty was somehow punishment due to God's disfavor. But Jesus taught that our wealth, social standing and good deeds have little to do with whether we will see God in heaven. Putting our hope in earthly wealth or an impressive record of good deeds will amount to nothing. Rather, the only ones who will see God are those with a pure heart, those who walk with him as Master and friend, those whose sins have been washed away by the blood of the Lamb.

Since "all have sinned and fall short of the glory of God,"[9] who, then, can purify our hearts for this sweet communion with God? The answer appears in the window's second inscription, toward the bottom just below the cloud, from John 11:25: "I am the Resurrection and the Life." This was Jesus' famous response to his friend Martha, moments before he would raise her brother Lazarus from the dead. Jesus demonstrates his extraordinary power over death first by restoring Lazarus to life, and second by promising to resurrect all those who believe him. The Resurrection at the end of the age will usher in an eternity of perfect fellowship between God and his people. Many will recall this verse as the opening line of our Burial of the Dead in the *Book of Common Prayer*.[10]

The third inscription, Revelation 2:10, appears in Greek circumscribed about the scepter and crown in the center panel: γινου πιστος αχρι θανατου και δωσω σοι τον στεφανον της ζωης , which means, "Be faithful unto death, and I will give you the crown of life." With these words, Jesus assures us of a glorious reward in heaven if we endure to the end. The promised reward is not something we earn, as if God owes us anything; rather, it is a gift from a gracious Father who asks us to trust him during times of sorrows and trials, even if we cannot humanly comprehend our sufferings. The hymnist reminds us that if we endure faithfully, we will one day be "created again that our lives may remain throughout time and eternity [the Lord's]" in Heaven.[11]

---

9   Romans 3:23.
10 Book of Common Prayer, pg. 469.
11 "Come Away to the Skies," *1982 Hymnal*, no. 213.

As we move up the window directly above the human images, the Communion paten and golden chalice remind us that Jesus is the Bread of Life, our sustainer from day to day[12], and the Blood of the New Covenant, our preserver for all eternity[13]. Just above are two budded crosses overlaid by the Alpha and the Omega[14], the first and last letters of the ancient Greek alphabet, a symbolic way of referring to Christ as Author and Finisher of our faith. Faith is not something that we achieve, but it comes as a gift from God, St. Paul tells us.[15] Jesus is also the Author of human history from beginning to end: "[A]ll things were made through him, and without him was not anything made that was made."[16] In the center panel are the scepter and crown, together a symbol of Christ's ultimate and permanent reign over all creation after he returns. The dove clasping an olive branch reminds us that Jesus is the Prince of Peace, the only One in all the universe who can reconcile us to the loving Father with whose fellowship we have broken by our sins[17], by forgiving our sins[18].

At the apex of the arch is the Head of the Church, the "IHS," the first three letters of the Greek word for "Jesus." It is accentuated by two lilies—a triple symbol of Christ's holiness, Nellie's youthful purity, and the resurrection to come. Note the tiny ears of wheat encircling the upper half of the center panel and flanking the Agnus Dei. In Matthew 9:38, Jesus calls himself the Lord of the harvest, who sends out laborers into the wheat fields to gather for himself a people, which will result in a day of great celebration.

The Story of the Family

Nellie Rathburn was 16 years old when she died on December 16, 1872. She is the only St. Paul's communicant whose image is depicted in the church's stained glass, with the possible exception of the Kidd Baptismal Window. She is buried at Beech Grove Cemetery in Pomeroy, Ohio, her mother's native town.

---

12 John 6:35.
13 I Corinthians 11:25.
14 Revelation 1:8.
15 Ephesians 2:8.
16 John 1:3.
17 Colossians 1:20.
18 Matthew 9:1-8.

William Perry Rathburn, Nellie's father and a leading businessman, was a two-term mayor of Chattanooga in 1870 and 1871 during Reconstruction, in the years following the War Between the States. He was also the Chamber of Commerce's first president. He served as a St. Paul's vestryman from 1876 until 1884. Mr. Rathburn was born in Rutland, Ohio, on February 12, 1822. He married Miss Catherine Whiton Daniel of Pomeroy, Ohio, in 1855 and came to Chattanooga in 1865, when he organized the First National Bank.
His biography states he was the first man who brought any considerable capital to Chattanooga after the close of the war and was connected with a great many enterprises which helped to build up the town. He was one of the Public Library's first and largest contributors in its formative period. He died in 1884 and apparently was buried at Beech Grove Cemetery in Pomeroy, Ohio (where a tombstone still stands) before being reinterred in 1887 at Forest Hills Cemetery, St. Elmo.

Catherine Whiton Daniel Rathburn, his widow, replaced her husband as a bank director due to her business acumen and pleasing personality and so remained for many years. During the Great Depression of the 1930s, after failures, reorganizations and consolidations, the remainder of First National Bank was absorbed by the American National Bank, itself being absorbed by SunTrust in more recent years. Mrs. Rathburn died on March 20, 1910, at the family home at the corner of Sixth and Pine streets.

Annie Grace Rathburn Nottingham, Nellie's sister, was a devoted member of St. Paul's for many years. She became wife of Mr. C.C. (Clarence Crawford) Nottingham, a leading manufacturer and businessman at the turn of the 20th century, who served as vice president of First National Bank in its later years. The Rathburn family died out in Chattanooga with Mrs. Nottingham's death on December 3, 1939, at the age of 72. Her family's handsome antebellum residence next door to the church, for many years one of the city's few surviving period houses and for nearly a century the site of important civic and social gatherings that helped to cultivate Chattanooga's reputation for hospitality and social charm, was demolished in the 1960s to make way for St. Barnabas Apartments and Nursing Home.

Windows one and two (of five) –
Design: Willet Stained Glass Studios, Philadelphia, 1997

4. Clerestory (Gospel Side)

Alexander Parable Windows

Will the World Come to an End?

Does anyone really know what the end of time will be like? Jesus did, and he used simple parables to give us a glimpse of the mysteries surrounding the cataclysmic events that will rock the world when he returns. Ironically, He also used parables to conceal their meaning from those who would not believe. Many of His parables begin with the phrase, "The kingdom of heaven is like ..." Through parables, Jesus taught that there is an afterlife, and in the courtroom of Judgment Day, every one of us must answer to God for our every thought, word and action. Because God is all-knowing, no stone will be left unturned—everything from the most heinous crime to the most idle word will be laid bare by the Judge of Heaven. The time is coming, Jesus warned, when "he shall stand at the [last] day upon the earth";[1] turn back to the loving Father before it is too late. "Repent, for the kingdom of heaven is at hand."[2]

In the clerestory on the Gospel (west) side of the nave are five stained glass lancet windows that depict 15 of Jesus' parables about the kingdom of heaven. Very modern in style and composed of large, one-inch thick pieces of *dalle de verre* glass set into wrought iron, these windows give off a jewel-like vibrancy in rich colors of red, blue, green, yellow, purple, gray and orange. They were given by Thomas D. Alexander (1917-98), a longtime member of St. Paul's and organist-choirmaster for 17 years. They were designed and installed by Willet Stained Glass Studios of Philadelphia and were dedicated on

---

1 *Book of Common Prayer*, 469.
2 Matthew 4:17.

*Windows three, four and five (of five) –
Design: Willet Stained Glass Studios, Philadelphia, 1997*

October 12, 1997. They replaced five amber glass windows which the Vestry resolved in the 1940s to keep because the afternoon sunlight was so lovely streaming into the sanctuary. This was before new modern lighting was installed in recent years.

All five widows share an identical border and field design. Each window contains three vertically aligned medallions, and each medallion bears a thumbnail sketch of a parable. The peculiar beauty of these windows lies in how simply and concisely each parable is expressed.

The Story in the Window

Let us glance at each parable, moving left to right, from the bell tower toward the high altar.

First window, closest to the bell tower:
- The top medallion shows the **parable of the sower** (found in Matthew 13:18-30; Mark 4:3-9; Luke 8:5-8). It describes the four universal reactions of people when Jesus' message of judgment and deliverance is proclaimed. The farmer (God) sows his seed (His message) in many different types of ground (human ears). Some seeds fall along the path (those who receive it with a closed mind or who fail to understand); others fall along the rocky soil (those who welcome it at first but then turn away due to hardship or embarrassment); still others fall along thorns (those who receive it for a short time but then are distracted by worldly comforts, wealth or possessions); finally there are those seeds that fall on fertile soil (those who hear the word of God with an open mind, understand it and put it into practice), yielding a productive crop (a beautiful life lived in joyful submission to God and service to others).

- The middle medallion shows the **parable of the houses on rock and on sand** (found in Matthew 7:24-27; Luke 6:48-49). It describes the two kinds of faith: Either our faith is built securely on Jesus' promises and commands (the rock) or it rests unsteadily on temporal things like wealth, power, modern medicine or the stock market (sand). When events such as depression, hardship, sickness or death hit us, those whose faith is built on the Rock will weather the storm, while those whose faith is built on sand will come crashing down in the end.

- The bottom medallion shows the **parable of the lost sheep** (found in Matthew 18:12-14; Luke 15:4-7), in which the compassionate shepherd leaves his 99 sheep on the hillside in search of the one lost sheep that has wandered off. In the same way, our heavenly Father has an active, pursuing love of each one of his children, particularly those who may be straying. The lost sheep could be any one of us at any time.

Second window, going toward the high altar:
- The top medallion shows the **parable of new wine in old wineskins** (found in Matthew 9:16-17; Mark 2:18-22; Luke 5:36-39). If new, unfermented wine is placed in old, stretched-out wineskins, the skins will burst, and the wine will be spilled. In the same way, it is possible for us to be so set in our ways and so fond of our traditions (old wineskins) that our minds cannot accept Jesus' radical warnings about God's kingdom to come (new wine), where the Lord will "purge this land of bitter things," as the hymnist reminds us.[3]

- The middle medallion shows the **parable of the wise and foolish virgins** (found in Matthew 25:1-13). This is one of several parables that describe Jesus' second coming, which He compared to an ancient marriage banquet. Jesus warned us to be watchful and ready for His return, which could happen at any moment. Jesus (the bridegroom) might take so long to arrive that His so-called friends (the guests) would grow drowsy waiting. When He finally will arrive, some of us will have used the time to prepare ourselves (the five wise virgins with lamps full of oil) while others will have lived as though that day would never come (the five foolish virgins with empty lamps). Only those who are ready for Jesus at His return will enter heaven (the great banquet). Those who are not ready will not be permitted to enter, as in the parable.

---

[3] "Judge Eternal, Enthroned in Splendor" *1982 Hymnal*, no. 596.

- The bottom medallion shows the **parable of the pearl of great price** (found in Matthew 13:45-46). This parable teaches the great price that God the Father places on His children: He sold His only Son to death on a cross to purchase a place for us in heaven. Our sin cost Him dearly (empty money pouch), but His love is greater than our sin. Another way to read this parable is how we should respond after recognizing what Christ did for us: Are we so overcome with gratitude and joy that we are willing to exchange everything we hold dear—riches, comforts, jobs, or our very lives—for Him (the pearl)? The extent to which we either give up or cling to these things will reveal the depth of our relationship with Him.

Third window, going toward the high altar:
- The top medallion shows the **parable of the mustard seed** (found in Matthew 13:31-32; Mark 4:31-32; Luke 13:18-19). This parable teaches that as long as our faith is placed in something eternal (Christ), any amount of faith is enough to reconcile us to God—even if our faith is weak or as tiny as a mustard seed! God can water that faith and produce a large tree that offers a resting place to the birds (hurting people). But if we place our faith in something fleeting (our family heritage, our charitable giving, our church membership, etc.), then can any amount of faith in these things save us from our sins on the day Christ returns?

- The middle medallion shows the **parable of the good Samaritan** (found in Luke 10:30-37). The Samaritans were half-Israelite, half-pagan—considered second-class citizens in Jesus' day because they were an embarrassing reminder of the Assyrian captivity 500 years earlier, in which Israelites were forcibly mixed with the surrounding peoples. So for the priest and the Levite—considered the most "righteous" people of their day (symbolically reduced to size in the background)—to walk on by while the "unclean" Samaritan stops to help the bruised traveler would have struck his audience as preposterous! He bandages the man's wounds and offers water and lodging. This parable was told in response to the one who asked Jesus, "Teacher, what shall I do to inherit eternal life?" As much as you love yourself, so you must love the one who most repulses you, Jesus responded. "[D]o this, and you will live."

- The bottom medallion shows the **parable of the full net** (found in Matthew 13:47-48). This parable teaches that all kinds of people are invited to be part of God's church on earth, just as a fisherman pulls to shore all kinds of fish inside his net. But on the day of judgment when the Lord makes all things known, he will identify those who are truly his (good fish) and those who aren't (bad fish).

Fourth window, going toward the high altar:
- The top medallion shows the **parable of the friend at midnight** (found in Luke 11:5-8). It teaches how willing and eager God is to receive those who seek him wholeheartedly. If an aroused neighbor will grant an unreasonable request (borrowing bread in the middle of the night) simply due to the asker's boldness, how much more will our generous Father hear our prayers and grant us the most reasonable request of all: sweet communion with those who seek him with all their hearts, with all their soul, and with all their strength! "[K]nock, and it will be opened to you ... ," this parable concludes.

- The middle medallion shows the **parable of the rich fool** (found in Luke 12:16-21). It illustrates the utter foolishness of hoarding wealth in this life—whether a house full of heirlooms, a schedule full of engagements, or a portfolio full of over-performing investments. How many of us are so busy tending to our worldly valuables (building bigger barns) that we have little left for the work God has called us to do (being rich toward God)? "Fool! This night your soul is required of you" (notice the bolt of lightning). In the end, when such a person will lose everything he held dear, what will he have to show for his life?

- The bottom medallion shows the **parable of the barren fig tree** (found in Luke 13:6-9). It illustrates that God is exceedingly patient with us—to a point. Year after year the master comes to his fig tree expecting a tasty harvest but is disappointed. Finally he orders it cut down (the axe). "[W]hy should it use up the ground?" he asks. His hired hand pleads for one more chance, promising to dig around the base of the tree (shovel) and fertilize it in hopes of bearing fruit. The master relents, but time is running out for the barren fig tree. How about us—are we bearing fruit that is pleasing to our Master, or are we just taking up space in His creation and testing God's patience?

Fifth window, closest to the high altar:
- The top medallion shows the **parable of laborers in the vineyard** (found in Matthew 20:1-16). Some laborers worked all day while others worked one hour (multiple clocks telling different times). Yet the master paid them identical wages. Those who had toiled all day are now jealous of those who worked a single hour. But the master reminds them, Have I acted unfairly? Did you not agree to your wages? We are reminded that as our sovereign Creator, God reserves every right to bless each one as he wishes—some with more, others with less. How fortunate we are to receive anything at all! Ought we to complain when others receive more? Another lesson from this parable is that rewards in the afterlife may not correspond tit-for-tat with how much "good" we think we've done on earth. Rather, any rewards we receive are based solely on God's good pleasure and incalculable generosity.

- The middle medallion shows the **parable of the talents** (found in Matthew 25:14-30; Luke 19:12-27). God (the master) has blessed each one of us to varying degrees. To some he gives great abundance (five talents), to others a modest sum (two talents), and to others just enough (one talent). On the day of reckoning, much accounting will be required from the person who received much in this lifetime (now 10 talents), and less from the one who received less (now four talents). But the one who feels justified in wasting God's gifts, choosing instead to bury with a shovel what little he received, will be punished for his laziness and impunity. Jesus says this man's destiny is hell, and what little he had will be turned over to the one who labored most faithfully. While this parable can be readily applied to finances, Jesus applied it more generally to everything God gives us. Are we using everything at our disposal—skills, opportunities and influence—to serve God, to love our neighbor, and to advance His kingdom? Or, like the unfaithful servant, have we buried them so that they are rendered useless? The Owner is coming back to reclaim these talents which rightly belong to him; what will we have to show for the way we used his generous gifts?

- The bottom medallion shows the **parable of the unmerciful servant** (found in Matthew 18:23-34). The king had ordered one of his servant-laborers to be sold to settle a large debt (hands holding stacks of gold). The servant pleaded for his life, and so the king forgave the debt. Now the debt-free servant-laborer turns on a fellow servant (shown by the jail bars and cat o' nine tails for whipping criminals) for what turns out to be a tiny debt (small money bag). This enrages the king, who now rescinds the mercy he had once shown to the ungrateful servant. This parable teaches how great is God's mercy to those who have sinned and how generously he forgives if we approach him in repentance and humility. It also teaches the extent to which we are called to show mercy to others—in light of the much greater mercy that God has shown to us. Have we been offended or insulted? Jesus forgave us, so we must forgive. Have we been denied something which rightly belongs to us? Jesus forgave us, so we must forgive. Have we been victimized by violence, oppression or theft? God leaves us with no wiggle room here either: Jesus forgave us, so we must forgive. For the extent to which we either show mercy or hold grudges against those who have harmed us, God will show the same to us on His day of judgment.

The Story of the Family

Thomas D. Alexander was St. Paul's organist and choirmaster from 1949 to 1966. Born on March 29, 1917, he graduated from Baylor School and the University of Tennessee at Chattanooga. He was married to Ruth Vander Maaten Alexander and was retired as a public school teacher from Duval County, Fla. At the time of his death on August 18, 1998, he left a sister, Mildred Lusk, of East Ridge, and a nephew, Thomas Lusk, of Huntsville, Ala.

Design: Artist unknown, 1892

5. St. George's Chapel

Staley Window

Would a Loving God Allow Suffering and Evil?

One of the great tragedies in St. Paul's parish history is memorialized in the Staley window in St. George's Chapel. Installed around 1892 and the first window specifically commissioned for the present building, this fine example of Victorian glass includes a combination of stained and painted glass. Its brilliant colors notwithstanding, a black wood encasement and coffin-like design lend this window a doleful look. One of only four in the church without a human image depicted, the window tells the story of sweet fellowship cruelly cut off. It was given in memory of young Jane Martha Staley by the St. Agnes Guild, of which she was an active member, who died on what should have been a joyous Easter Sunday 1891, after a tragic shooting accident in her sister's home. Miss Staley's personal tragedy reflects the greatest tragedy in all human history: Mankind's sweet fellowship with our Heavenly Father cruelly cut off in the Garden of Eden, and the violent price His Son paid on the cross to restore it. Ironically, it is the only stained glass window in the church to have witnessed suffering of its own as it was seriously damaged during an attempted break-in on January 18, 1978.

The Story in the Window

Like the Chapman window in the clerestory above, the Staley window reminds us that life on earth is presently not all it was meant to be. In the beginning, we were designed by our Creator to live forever in beautiful fellowship with one another and with Him. But something went horribly wrong: hate ... abuse ... murder ... dishonesty ... discrimination ... unfaithfulness ... pollution ... greed ... war ... death. How could a loving God allow things to get so out of control?

He didn't, *we* did! In Genesis, God generously gave Adam and Eve a garden paradise filled with rich foods, dazzling flora and friendly animals. He entrusted them as stewards to care for the creation and exercise dominion over it. As if that were not enough, God walked intimately alongside them as a loving Father, friend and guide. But our first parents turned their backs on their loving Creator, setting their affections on the only thing that God made off limits: "You may freely eat of every tree of the garden; but of the tree of the knowledge of good and evil you shall not eat, for in the day that you eat of it you shall die."[1] As they satisfied their craving against their Father's warning, immediately their hearts were poisoned against Him (and one another), and their bodies became subject to decay. As a little yeast that works its way through the whole batch of dough, our first parents' rebellious spirit spread to the rest of their descendants, and we all have lived under their curse of suffering and death ever since. "The wages of sin is death," St. Paul told us.[2]

But God loved us too much to let us go our own way forever, and he set out to make things right, strangely enough through an even greater tragedy than the first. He gave up his innocent, perfect Son so that by his sufferings, ours would end. By cheating death and rising from the tomb, Jesus Christ overcame both tragedies with one mighty act. The Staley window comforts us in our suffering with God's promise of fellowship restored—not only with our loved ones, but primarily with Himself. As the hymnist reminds us (No. 358), heaven will be a place where "Grief and pain [are] ended, and sighing no longer."[3] This window serves as a reminder that while grief and pain are real, Jesus' ultimate suffering for our sake will one day will bring an end to our own suffering.

The window is composed of four tall lancet arches subsumed under a horizontal basket arch. The two inner lancets are nearly identical,

---

1 Genesis 2:15-17.
2 Romans 6:23.
3 "Christ the Victorious, Give to Your Servants" 1982 Hymnal, no. 358.

as are the two outer ones. The dominant colors are red and white, representing our present suffering and our future purity, respectively. These are laced with gold, blue and green throughout.

In the core of the outer lancets on a blue field are two golden monograms representing the name of Jesus Christ in Greek. Early Christians used a number of shorthand abbreviations when referring to our Lord or communicating who He was. From Greek it is an abbreviation of the name ΙΗΣΟΥΣ (Jesus) ΧΡΙΣΤΟΣ (Christ). Usually we would expect to see this shortened to *IHS XPS*; but here it is expressed in its alternate form as *IHS XPC*, where the final character is a moon-shaped S known as a *lunate sigma* that resembles a C[4]. Above and below each monogram we see a *fleur-de-lis*, or iris, which carries multiple meanings but here is best understood as a representation of purity: Jesus' wounds cover our sins so that we can stand pure before our Father again. Capping each outer panel is a long stem red rose, which speaks to the Father's immeasurable love for us that he would sentence His Son to death to bring our sufferings to an end. We know that Christ is present in the midst of every tragedy, walking alongside us in faith through the valley of the shadow of death, until we are made pure and restored to Him in the heavenly places.

The inner lancets focus on an arrangement of calla lilies, often seen adorning graves and, therefore, associated with somber mourning. At the same time, this beautiful flower is another emblem of purity. It is a fitting tribute to the woman whose life was cut short in the flower of her youth.

Emblazoned over the lilies are Jesus' consoling words from his Sermon on the Mount, "Blessed are the pure in heart, for they shall see God."[5] Those who have been purified by Jesus' suffering will enjoy eternal fellowship with God. Notice how the lilies appear to blot out the blood red background, reminding us that Jesus came to earth to "dry the tears of those who weep."[6] Below the lilies are two empty Tudor arches, perhaps to signify the void which earthly

---

4 http://oxforddictionaries.com/us/definition/american_english/sigma
5 Matthew 5:8.
6 Book of Common Prayer, 497.

suffering leaves in our ravaged souls. But these sufferings are capped by doves, to signify peace restored between God and mankind. Notice the doves' vertical orientation, sent down from above; it is God who restores our fellowship with him, and he did it through the suffering of Jesus Christ. Across the bottom of the window, the dedication inscription ends with the hopeful words, "Entered into rest Easter Day 1891."

The four lancets point heavenward, toward a constellation of round jewels set in blue rippled glass above the main body of the window. Amid the suffering and death we experience on earth, our eyes must be pointed upward to the treasure that awaits us in the heavenly realms, where our fellowship with God and one another will be restored to its original purity and beauty—the way God designed it in the beginning.

The Story of the Family

Jennie Martha Staley was one of at least three daughters of the Rev. Thomas Jefferson Staley and Susan Martha Verdrey Staley, born in 1866. Her father was appointed by the Episcopal Church to minister at St. Stephen's Chapel in Savannah, Ga., believed to be the second parish established for African-Americans in the South. Her widowed mother moved the family to Chattanooga in 1870. A member of the St. Agnes Guild, young Jennie met tragedy on March 26, 1891, at the College Street home of her sister Gertrude (wife of Judge Hugh Whiteside, mayor from 1883 to 1885). Her untimely death, which shocked the city, is preserved in gory detail in a *Chattanooga Times* article:

> *Shortly after 7 o'clock Judge Whiteside removed from his pocket a 32-calibre revolver and laid it on a bureau in his bedroom. Inspired by womanly curiosity, Miss Staley, who was present, picked up the pistol to examine it. An instant later there was a sharp, explosive report, and Miss Staley fell back, shot in the left breast, with a faint streak of blood trickling down the front of her dress. Appalled at the terrible sight, Judge Whiteside picked up the unfortunate young lady in his arms and laid her tenderly on the bed ...*

At first the wound was reported to have missed all vital organs, but by the third day her demise appeared inevitable. A subsequent account reads:

> *Over a mother's grief and a sister's woe let the record be silent. Leave consolation for the bleeding hearts with Him from whose hands they came.*

She died three days later on Easter Sunday, March 29, 1891, the most celebrated day of the church calendar, and is buried at Forest Hills Cemetery, St. Elmo. Her mother was laid to rest beside her in 1925. Her sister Laura, who married Chattanooga pharmaceutical manufacturer Joseph Frederick Voigt and became the mother of Mrs. Joseph Howard Davenport, lived until 1953.

Judge Hugh Whiteside was Chattanooga's first native-born mayor, born on December 8, 1854, to Col. James A. Whiteside and Harriet L. Whiteside. He practiced law here for many years after graduating from the University of the South at Sewanee and Washington Law University at St. Louis. After serving as a city alderman (forerunner of today's city council), he was elected mayor for two terms from 1883 to 1885, afterward serving as an elected county judge for the remainder of his life. In 1880 he married Miss Gertrude Staley, sister of Jennie Martha Staley. Judge Whiteside's father, a Kentucky native, was one of Chattanooga's early settlers, moving here in 1840 and serving in the State Legislature. The Whitesides are one of Chattanooga's few pioneer families who still bear their original surname, as many First Families descendants still residing here are now represented by different surnames due to marriage. Judge Whiteside died on February 14, 1896, and is buried at Forest Hills Cemetery.

Design: Charles Foster, Chattanooga, 1928

5. St. George's Chapel

Garvin
St. George Window

How Generous Does God Expect Me to Be?

A rich young man once came to Jesus with a question that troubled him deeply: "Teacher, what good deed must I do, to have eternal life?"[1] Like the answer Jesus gave the rich young man, the imagery in the Garvin St. George window steers us into a commitment far larger than we may be ready to take on.

The Garvin St. George window is admittedly one of the most difficult to interpret; on the surface the artist has created a colorful mosaic of loose iconography, some more abstractly rendered than others. Yet below the surface is a compelling reminder of our Christian calling to be willing to sacrifice everything for the sake of others—without seeking credit or reward for ourselves.

It is an Art Nouveau memorial to Minnie Newman Garvin, who died on January 23, 1918. Mrs. Garvin was actively identified with numerous charitable endeavors within St. Paul's and in Chattanooga prior to and during World War I. Designed to give a warm glow to the yellow brick of the St. George's Chapel and to be in harmony with the adjacent Staley window, the Garvin St. George window was made by Charles Foster in Chattanooga in 1928.

---

1 Matthew 19:16.

The Story in the Window

In reply to the rich young man's excellent question, Jesus said,

> "Why do you ask me about what is good? One there is who is good. If you would enter life, keep the commandments." He said to him, "Which?" And Jesus said, "You shall not kill, You shall not commit adultery, You shall not steal, You shall not bear false witness, Honor your father and mother, and, You shall love your neighbor as yourself." The young man said to him, "All these I have observed; what do I still lack?" Jesus said to him, "If you would be perfect, go, sell what you possess and give to the poor, and you will have treasure in heaven; and come, follow me." When the young man heard this he went away sorrowful; for he had great possessions. And Jesus said to his disciples, "Truly, I say to you, it will be hard for a rich man to enter the kingdom of heaven."[2]

As one of the popular and cutting-edge art styles of the day, Art Nouveau emphasized natural forms and structures over strict representation of real-world objects. The style is largely focused on organic and curved lines; women and nature were both prominent subjects. Ultimately, Art Nouveau would lead to the abstract Modernist styles that would follow throughout the 20th Century.

While much of the symbolism in the upper portions of four lancets is abstract, the shapes and colors seem to resemble fruit and organic growth. The prominence of green throughout the window may be representative of steady and faithful growth.

At the heart of the window an inscription on two open scrolls bears the name of St. George, the chapel's namesake. One of the most venerated saints in all of Christendom and the patron saint of England, George was a crusading knight of the late third and early fourth centuries who was martyred for his bold declaration of Christ and refusal to bow to Rome's gods. While many stories of the feats of St. George survive, the most famous is of St. George and the

---

2   Matthew 19:17-23.

Dragon. According to legend, a town was terrorized by a dragon who demanded the sacrifice of a young maiden. St. George bravely charged into battle, willing to sacrifice all he had, to protect the young girl. St. George embodied generosity to the extreme, willing to sacrifice his life to protect one that was helpless and in need. Today, St. George is thought of as a symbol of gallant selflessness, putting others before himself and his own comfort and preservation.

Stylized fountains representing flowing good works may be what we see depicted across the top of all four lancet windows, though a precise identification is challenging; yet fountains nicely fit the narrative. They pour into other fountains; symbolizing fresh water to weary travelers and hospitality—two good works celebrated throughout Scripture. We think of Rachel watering Jacob's camels, or the Samaritan woman offering Jesus a cool drink. The fountain has represented both refreshment of the weary, the pouring of life into others, and mercy for the poor. This symbolism would seem appropriate for Mrs. Garvin's service with the Red Cross—tending to wounded soldiers in distant battlefields with little recognition. The acorns from strong oak trees symbolize the strength lent from one to another in good works.

Pink roses blooming off the top of the fountains crown each lancet. Why? Truly good works are done out of love—the love of God, not the praise of others, or even for self-satisfaction. Love of God is the only incentive or motivation for truly good works.

Surrounding these good works are the Alpha and Omega, the first and last letters of the Greek alphabet, inscribed into the outer panels in their Anglicized forms as "A" and "O." In Revelation 22:13, Jesus says, "I am the Alpha and the Omega, the first and the last, the beginning and the end." In wondering how generous we ought to be, we are reminded that good works are not, strictly speaking, something *we* do; rather, they originate with God's plan, flourish in God's power, and find their fulfillment in God's purposes. How often have we found ourselves overly impressed by our own good works, or striving to accumulate enough good deeds to earn public recognition or please God? Aren't they *God's* works to begin with, accomplished *through* us, not *by* us? Unless we are willing to pour ourselves out as a fountain on behalf of those in need, have we really been generous enough? Can we ever out-give Jesus, who poured out his life as a fountain for the sins of many? Compared to his sacrifice, how our own generosity pales in comparison!

The Story of the Family

Minnie Newman Garvin was an early St. Paul's communicant who was actively identified with numerous organizations within the church. She was noted for her work with the Red Cross and the National League of Woman's Services[3], particularly during World War I. Founded in 1917 in conjunction with the Red Cross, the National League provided stateside for veterans, ensuring they received food and lodging during their travels and deployment.

> *In Mrs. Garvin's death Chattanooga loses a noble woman, than whom none were more esteemed in a community she ennobled by her grace and by her splendid womanhood. She was endowed with that high order of patriotism that found expression in genuine service. She was imbued with the highest ambition of wifehood and motherhood. She was gifted with strong intelligence and remarkable industry. Since America's declaration of war Mrs. Garvin has been prominent in the noble band of women who have rendered substantial service. She served the cause well and faithful and in every movement of patriotism. In every activity of merciful usefulness looking to the comfort of soldiers here at home and soldiers abroad this woman has been zealous in every local endeavor. Ever earnest in her purpose to fulfill the obligations of life in her home, in society and in deeds of charity and mercy, she typified in all things modesty, honor and fidelity and won her place in the affections of all who were honored by acquaintance. She was esteemed because the gentleness of her soul measured up to the strength and vigor of her mind.*

---

3 http://brooklynology.brooklynpubliclibrary.org/post/2010/07/29/National-League-of-Womens-Services.aspx (paragraph 2).

She was born on November 17, 1862, in Crystal Springs, Miss., and later married D. Cal. McMillin (1865-1893). Her two sons, Douglass Newman McMillin (d. 1951) and Edwyn West McMillin (d. 1988), were young Army officers stationed at Camp Sevier in Greenville, S.C., at the time of her death on January 23, 1918. She and her husband are buried at Forest Hills Cemetery, St. Elmo.

Judge Walter Brown Garvin, her second husband, was a widely respected jurist in the Tennessee Chancery Court. A schoolteacher in Missouri before entering the field of law, Judge Garvin was appointed to the court by Governor Thomas C. Rye in 1916, before running for election in 1918 and again in 1926. He was preparing to announce his candidacy for another eight-year term when he died on January 27, 1934, at age 72.

> *On the bench the chancellor was strictly business. The bar respected him, his honesty and integrity and his ability [was] never questioned in any quarter. So often were his opinions affirmed by the appellate courts of this state that he became to be known through Tennessee as the judge whose judgment and skill in arriving at legal conclusions stood highest.*

He is buried beside his wife at Forest Hills Cemetery.

Design: Artist unknown, 1916

6. NAVE

DAVIDSON-BROWN WINDOW

Why Can't We All Get Along?

Many might remember Rodney King's famous national plea at the height of the 1992 Los Angeles race riots: "Can we all get along?" Getting along seems so simple ... so why can't we? The Bible says there's something cross-wired inside every one of us that makes the Golden Rule very hard to follow. We often think of ourselves as mostly good except for one or two bad habits; or we might assume that except for a few bad apples, most of us are decent folks. But St. Paul saw things differently: "None is righteous, no, not one ... no one does good, not even one ... since all have sinned and fall short of the glory of God."[1] And precisely because we humans tend *not* to get along, God has filled Scripture with instructions on *how* to get along. The Davidson-Brown window, found on the main floor of the nave, reminds us of a time when the early Christians were not getting along—and how they addressed a controversy that threatened to split the young church.

The Davidson-Brown window is on the epistle side of the nave, just beyond St. George's Chapel toward the high altar. Designed in a very high Victorian style, this window has an effusion of gothic tracery and architecture, most prominently on display at the top and bottom of each panel. These include arches, chapels, turrets and crosses. The window contains both stained and painted glass. It opens onto an air shaft between the nave, the Ava Wright Room and St. George's Chapel, with colors of blue, green, yellow, cream, red, rose, grey and black.

---

1   Romans 3:10, 12, 23.

Installed in 1916, the window was given by Mr. and Mrs. Edward Davidson in memory of his father, mother and sister: "Sacred to the memory of Mr. and Mrs. C.A. Davidson and daughter Mattie Davidson Brown." An unknown English studio is credited with its design.

The Story in the Window

The story found in the Davidson-Brown window culminates in Acts 15:36-41. St. Paul and St. Barnabas were dear friends and partners in the gospel. It was Barnabas who won Paul over to the other apostles, who were still skeptical about this former arch-enemy of the church. It was Barnabas who accompanied Paul on his first missionary journey through the Greek world, where they were persecuted for their faith. And it was Barnabas who joined Paul in Jerusalem to settle a sharp debate which threatened to split the church. In Antioch, some believed that all Christians were bound by all the Old Testament ceremonial rules, such as abstaining from pork or circumcising infants; others disagreed. Who was right? Both sides agreed to argue their case before the apostles in Jerusalem and to abide by the decision. The hearing was held, and Barnabas and Paul returned with the ruling. The Bible tells us, "And when [the people] read it, they rejoiced at the exhortation."[2] Thus no one's view was imposed on the other, and the church remained unified in love.

Ironically, although the church was so harmoniously held together, a personal dispute now arose between the two friends over John Mark, a helper turned deserter. About to set out on his second missionary journey, Paul couldn't risk traveling with one who had proven unfit for service, but Barnabas believed in second chances. Acts 15:39-41 tells us, "And there arose a sharp contention, so that they separated from each other; Barnabas took Mark with him and sailed away to Cyprus, but Paul chose Silas and departed … And he went through Syria and Cilicia, strengthening the churches." In the window's center panel we see St. Paul in a yellow nimbus taking leave of Barnabas as the two saints go their separate ways in serving the Lord. Kneeling in the foreground is, we think, John Mark with hands clasped in sorrow over the division he has caused. Behind Paul is likely Silas, his new traveling

---

2 Acts 15:31.

companion. Above them looms the ship with its sails, masts and rigging which Barnabas and John Mark are about to board to Cyprus. Paul and Silas will travel on foot through Syria and Cilicia.

The figures in the two outer panels are harder to identify. Seeing as they mostly face away from the center, we might imagine these symbolically stress the fracture in the church's missionary movement caused by Paul and Barnabas' quarrel. In spite of personal division between the two missionary giants, the church's mission remained intact, as depicted by the continuity of the sky, sand and grass in the background shared by all three panels. However, since the window's focus is St. Paul, it's equally possible to conclude that these are the dear believers he met on his second missionary journey: St. Timothy and his parents (left) and St. Lydia and the women of Philippi (right).

And thus the Davidson-Brown window gives us the Bible's formula for getting along: Rather than impose our views on others, we must recognize our own tendency for *not* getting along, we submit to one another in love, and we place the church's mission above all else—even if it means not getting our way.

The Story of the Family

Charles Alexander Davidson, in whose memory the window is dedicated, was born in Aberdeen, Scotland, in 1832. In 1852 he immigrated to America, living in New York until 1869, when he came to Chattanooga. For a time he was connected with William Crutchfield's Dry Goods Store and later with the Roane Iron Co., a mining concern founded by  General (later Mayor) John T. Wilder, which produced the first steel to come out of the South. In 1881 he opened a men's fine clothier at the corner of Market and Eight streets, originally called Davidson & Son and later known as Davidson's Clothing Co. His was the first store in Chattanooga to have plate glass display windows, which drew much attention. A St. Paul's communicant, Mr. Davidson was elected to the vestry in 1893 and managed the store until his death on July 17, 1899.

Margaret Jane Mowbray Davidson, his wife, was born in 1829 and bore seven children. She was the sister of the Rev. William Mowbray, fifth rector of St. Paul's who served for a few months in 1859. She died on March 22, 1911, with a condition known as softening of the brain. She and her husband are buried at Forest Hills Cemetery, St. Elmo.

Edward Davidson followed in his father's footsteps, himself a prominent merchant on Market Street for 40 years. He was born in Chattanooga, where he lived all his life except for six months spent in Butte, Mont., where he joined his brothers in the wholesale grocery business. He returned to Chattanooga and joined his father's firm with his brother and was active in the business until he became ill. Eighteen months later, at the age of 60, he died at his home in Riverview on November 5, 1931. The funeral was held at the residence by Dr. Oliver J. Hart, rector of St. Paul's, assisted by the Rev. Thomas S. McCallie, who was chaplain of the city, brother of McCallie School's co-founders, and minister of Central Presbyterian Church. Edward Davidson was survived by his widow; a daughter, Mrs. Robert Renfro of New York; a son, Charles A. Davidson of Chattanooga, named for his grandfather; and two brothers, Roger M. Davidson and Robert Davidson, both of Boise, Idaho. He is buried at Forest Hills Cemetery.

Mattie Davidson Brown, sister of Edward Davidson, was born in 1865. She was the first wife of C. Victor Brown, long-time real estate entrepreneur and one of a group of land investors who developed Highland Park, one of Chattanooga's earliest suburbs, beginning in 1887. They were married on January 17, 1888. She was active at Second Presbyterian Church. A newspaper article at the time characterized her as follows:

> *Even as a child she possessed the most lovable temperament imaginable. At school she was a universal favorite, a girl to whom her companions unconsciously went for advice and consolation in their little school girl troubles, which seemed at that time to be great ones, however, the deeper sorrow of life being unknown. These sympathetic and lovable qualities of mind and heart accompanied her through her youth and into her womanhood. Indeed, her marriage brought out into bolder relief and accentuated these womanly graces and made them sweeter still.*

She died on March 20, 1894, at home at 317 Cedar St. and was buried at Forest Hills Cemetery. She left four young daughters under the age of 6.

C. Victor Brown, her widowed husband, was for many years a leading civic organizer, real estate entrepreneur and church leader in our city. He came to Chattanooga in 1881 at the age of 19, one of seven children born to Jacob N. and Sarah McCutcheon Brown of Adams County, Ohio. He became a partner in 1886 with Sam Divine and Henry Trent Olmsted in the Southern Land and Loan Company. This was before the days of TVA dams, so growing concern with frequent flooding of the Tennessee River piqued the interest of citizens seeking an escape to higher ground. Purchasing a $7,600 tract of land from a friend that was both up from the river's lower flood plains and away from the bustle and heat of downtown, they cleared and platted present-day Highland Park. In February 1887, the Highland Park Improvement Co. arranged to develop the property and Brown's company prepared for an early summer auction. Running trains on Charles E. James' belt line to attract a large crowd, the auction was a great success, selling every lot at a profit of $11,200.[3] Later, with his brother in the C.V. Brown & Bro. real estate firm, Mr. Brown developed other properties, including the old Keystone Block, bordered by Georgia Avenue and Cherry Street, which housed one of the city's early luxury office buildings, the first with an elevator. He served as president of the Chamber of Commerce, president of the park commission, and treasurer of the city's first street car company. But he devoted the majority of his civic efforts to Second Presbyterian Church and its Sunday school program, serving for 36 years as an officer. The Founders Memorial annex across Pine Street from St. Paul's was constructed under Mr. Brown's 23-year watch as Sunday school superintendent. Mr. Brown's descendants, many of them still in Chattanooga, are the issue of his second marriage, to Miss Catherine Keith Colburn, daughter of Maj. Webster Jay Colburn and Ada Elizabeth Brabson Colburn in 1896, two years following the death of his first wife, Mattie Davidson Brown. It was this second Mrs. Brown who, in 1908, conceived the idea of Signal Mountain's Little Brown Church (Union Chapel). Mr. Brown succumbed to heart disease on November 23, 1929, at his home at 835 Vine St. and is buried at Forest Hills Cemetery.

---

3 Cullon Hooks, "Highland Park Historic Resources Survey," September 30, 2005.

Windows one, two and three (of six) –
Design of One: Pennsylvania's Pittsburgh Stained Glass Studios and
C.Z. Lawrence Stained Glass, 1992.
Design of Two & Three: thought to be Payne Studio in Patterson, N.J., 1920s.

7. Apse

NIELAND-OVERMYER MUSICAL ANGELS WINDOWS

Do Angels Watch over Us?

Do angels exist? Are they watching over us? While angels may shape our lives more than we suspect, we probably give them more attention than they warrant. How apt, then, that they look down at us from the highest point in the nave—the lancet windows in the roof above the high altar—where they are removed from our direct line of sight. These six exquisite musical angels are adaptations in stained glass of 12 late medieval musical angels painted by Fra Angelico (ca. 1400-53) in the convent church of San Marco in Florence, Italy. It is thought that the center four were made in the renowned Payne Studio in Patterson, N.J., and installed in the late 1920s. They were given by Mrs. Francis Nieland as memorials to her mother Marion A. Carlile, father Thomas J. Carlile, husband Francis Nieland and herself.

Through a gift from Ruth E. Overmyer, the four original musical angel lancets were restored in 1991 and dedicated on June 14, 1992. At the same time, two of the four original amber glass windows, which flank the first four angel lancets, were replaced with new angel windows in memory of Donald H. Overmyer, her husband. Styled after the originals, these were made by Pennsylvania's Pittsburgh Stained Glass Studios and C.Z. Lawrence Stained Glass, and the two remaining end windows were renewed to match their background.

The drapery of the angels is particularly remarkable. The amber background, with its small pieces of fine stained glass, is styled after

Windows four, five and six (of six) –
Design of Four & Five: thought to be Payne Studio in Patterson, N.J., 1920s.
Design of Six: Pennsylvania's Pittsburgh Stained Glass Studios and
C.Z. Lawrence Stained Glass, 1992.

the gold leaf found in the paintings of the angels in Florence. Each of the angels holds a 15th century musical instrument: we see (left to right) a tambourine, trumpet, lyre, viol (forebear of the violin), second trumpet and drum. As each window is 8 feet tall, the life-sized angels are much larger than they appear from below.

The Story in the Window

Angels are ministering spirits created by God before humans. They exist first to surround God with songs of joyous praise. As the seasonal hymn reminds us, "Angels from the realms of glory, wing your flight o'er all the earth; ye who sang creation's story, now proclaim Messiah's birth."[1] It is symbolically appropriate that our six musical angel windows are positioned at the highest point of our church building, looking down onto the high altar as if from heaven. We are reminded of the important role of angels each week in The Great Thanksgiving when the celebrant says,

> *Therefore we praise you, joining our voices with Angels and Archangels and with all the company of heaven, who for ever sing this hymn to proclaim the glory of your Name …*[2]

We, his people, form part of this great cosmic company that will forever sing his praise not only for all the wonders he has done but also for the wonder that he is. The most famous angel is Gabriel, who announced the Messiah's birth to the Virgin Mary in Luke 1, followed by the angelic chorus that appeared to the shepherds in the next chapter. This event was known as the Enunciation, which we celebrate on March 25. The angels in the Nieland-Overmyer windows remind us of these with their musical instruments in hand. We see in these instances that another important role of angels is to announce messages from God to men. The Greek word *angelos* means "messenger."

Should we be scared of angels? Yes and no. Those who love God wholeheartedly have nothing to fear, for angels are ministering spirits

---
1 "Angels, from the realms of glory" *1982 Hymnal,* no. 93.
2 *Book of Common Prayer,* 362.

sent by God to guard his people[3], to meet our needs[4], and to rescue us from trouble: "The angel of the Lord encamps around those who fear him, and delivers them"[5]. Yet we are warned not to grow too spiritually intimate with angels: St. Paul instructs us not to worship or pray to angels[6], for God alone deserves our worship—and because someday we ourselves will rule over the angels[7].

As for those who neither walk with God nor love him wholeheartedly, angels should be feared; the book of Revelation says that angels will be the last faces to be seen as they are led away to judgment.[8] While at times we may wrestle with whether angels are real, St. Paul cautioned us to treat everyone graciously, particularly strangers, "for thereby some have entertained angels unawares."[9]

The Story of the Family

Thomas J. Carlile, born in 1833 in Philadelphia to Quaker parents, was a jewelry manufacturer and later a major in the Union Army. He was ordered to Chattanooga after the Battle of Chickamauga during the War Between the States. After the war, he became a successful businessman and a leading citizen. He was mayor from 1877 to 1878 and was a vestryman of St. Paul's. Major Carlile lived in a handsome Victorian house on West Ninth Street (now Martin Luther King Boulevard) about where the U.S. 27 overpass is now. During Chattanooga's yellow fever epidemic of 1878, Maj. Carlile chose to remain in the city tending to the sick, rather than flee for healthier climes as many did. He eventually contracted the disease himself and died that same year.

Marion A. Bendring Carlile, his wife, was born on May 22, 1838 in Pennsylvania. Their children were Walter Cope Carlile, Helen

---

3 Psalm 91:11; Hebrews 1:14.
4 I Kings 19:5-7; Matthew 4:11.
5 Psalm 34:7.
6 Colossians 2:18.
7 I Corinthians 6:3.
8 Revelation 8-9.
9 Hebrews 13:2.

A. Carlile and Cornelia Carlile (Mrs. James Reid). She died on November 18, 1926, and is buried at Chattanooga National Cemetery beside her husband.

Helen A. Carlile Nieland, their daughter, gave many memorials at St. Paul's, including the high altar of Italian marble in memory of her first husband, William W. Younge. As Mrs. Francis Nieland, she and her second husband lived in Washington, D.C., for many years. Perhaps her greatest gift to the parish was a large block of Coca-Cola stock bequeathed upon her death at age 72 on January 9, 1932, which became the Nieland Fund, the basis of St. Paul's Endowment. This is a trust in perpetuity whose principal is never to be spent and whose purpose is "the extension of the Kingdom"—helping God's people everywhere in the world. She is buried at Forest Hills Cemetery, St. Elmo.

Ruth Elberfeld Overmyer was a devoted member of St. Paul's and had been president of the parish Episcopal Church Women. With her friend of many years Ginny (Mrs. George) Power, also a St. Paul's parishioner, she was an avid tennis player and a Southern tennis champion. She was one of five sisters, all standout athletes. Their father, Norman "Kid" Elberfeld, had been an outstanding Major League Baseball player. Mrs. Overmyer was a graduate of the University of Chattanooga and a member of Pi Beta Phi sorority. Active in the community, she had been board president of Girls Preparatory School and a leader in the Chattanooga Girls Scouts. She and her husband had two children, Don H. Overmyer, Jr., and Susan Jane Overmyer Chandler. Mrs. Overmyer died on February 9, 1994, while playing tennis at her winter home in Naples, Fla.

Donald Howard Overmyer was a leading industrialist who had come to this city from Chicago in 1926 to play football for the University of Chattanooga. A local business and civic leader, he was an officer of local, state and national manufacturer associations, and a director of the American National Bank (now SunTrust). He served on the board of several companies, gave much of his time and energy to the United Fund (now United Way), and was a Rotarian and St. Paul's vestryman. It was said that Mr. Overmyer's gifts to St. Paul's were made quietly and always when needed most. He died on October 2, 1990.

The Stained Glass of St. Paul's

Design: Chapel Studios, London, 1983

8. Apse Corridor

Ellis Window

Why Wouldn't Jesus Save Himself?

Who could question the extraordinary impact of Jesus' brief life on centuries of human history? So it is hard not to wonder why, after Jesus spent three years preaching good news to the poor, healing the sick, restoring sight to the blind, calming violent storms, walking on water, raising the dead to life, captivating audiences and confounding enemies, he so passively allowed a runaway train of tragic events to cut his life short. Why would his detractors be allowed to say, "He saved others; he cannot save himself"?[1]

For three years Jesus had built an unprecedented following in Israel though his compassion for the poor and outcast, his authority over the Scriptures, and his fearlessness against the religious and political powers of his day. Rumors swirled: Might HE be the long-awaited Messiah who would deliver Israel from her Roman oppressors and restore King David's ancient throne? On Palm Sunday, his glorious moment had arrived; the nation seemed ready to crown him King! Yet in a single week, Jesus would be betrayed, abandoned, arrested, tried, mocked, beaten, stripped and executed—and the Bible tells us he did *absolutely nothing* to stop this dreadful sequence of events. Was his passivity part of a larger plan?

The Ellis window shows scenes from Holy Week, the dramatic final days of Jesus' earthly ministry, which are encapsulated by the inscription near the bottom from Job 19:25: *I know that my redeemer*

---

1 Matthew 27:42.

liveth. Colored in brown, tan, flesh, green, lilac, red, yellow and gray, the window was designed by Chapel Studios, London, and dedicated on the Day of Pentecost, Whitsunday, May 22, 1983, along with three others in the apse corridor behind the nave. It was given by Mr. and Mrs. Lewis F. Ellis, St. Paul's communicants. As the only window depicting Jesus' Resurrection—the climax and fulfillment of all God's promises in the Old Testament and the single historical event on which the entire Christian faith stands—one could easily imagine this window located in a more significant space, or perhaps on a larger wall.

The Story in the Window

> *He was oppressed, and he was afflicted,*
> * yet he opened not his mouth;*
> *like a lamb that is led to the slaughter,*
> * and like a sheep that before its shearers is dumb,*
> * so he opened not his mouth.*[2]

Holy Week began with such promise. At lower left we see Jesus' triumphal entry into Jerusalem riding on a donkey. Thousands of Jewish pilgrims were arriving for the annual Passover, a joyous feast commemorating the nation's deliverance from Egyptian slavery 1,500 years prior. As the great healer made his way into the city, cheering onlookers laid down palm fronds as a sign of reverence. The self-righteous religious leaders and Roman collaborators seethed as they witnessed the multitudes hailing, "Blessed is the King who comes in the name of the Lord!" Here is the historical origin of Palm Sunday, an event of such magnitude that it is recorded by all four gospel writers in Matthew 21, Mark 11, Luke 19 and John 12. Had Jesus sought to establish an earthly kingdom, surely this moment presented itself like no other!

But wait. At middle right we notice Jesus standing *silently* on trial before the Roman governor Pontius Pilate, representing a drastic turn of events five days later.

---

[2] Isaiah 53:7.

> *But when he was accused by the chief priests and elders, he made no answer. Then Pilate said to him, "Do you not hear how many things they testify against you?" But he gave him no answer, not even to a single charge; so that the governor wondered greatly.*[3]

Pilate, shown washing his hands of the injustice that is about to occur, cowardly bargains with the angry crowd for an opportunity to release their "King," whom they now seek to destroy: *Why, what evil has he done?*[4] The religious leaders have stirred their passions against Jesus, for he threatens their sense of self-righteousness and entitlement. Behind Jesus are Roman soldiers, ready to lead him away with savage beatings on a death march to the cross. The cross was a favorite execution device of the Romans. Jesus would not resist the soldiers, just as he had not resisted arrest in the Garden of Gethsemane the night before.

At middle left is Jesus' crucifixion, showing his grieving followers at Golgotha, the hill outside Jerusalem where Jesus was cruelly nailed to a wooden cross. Beside him are two criminals who were crucified for crimes which, unlike Jesus, they had actually committed.

> *One of the criminals who were hanged railed at him, saying, "Are you not the Christ? Save yourself and us!" But the other rebuked him, saying, "Do you not fear God, since you are under the same sentence of condemnation? And we indeed justly; for we are receiving the due reward of our deeds; but this man has done nothing wrong." And he said, "Jesus, remember me when you come into your kingdom." And he said to him, "Truly, I say to you, today you will be with me in Paradise."*[5]

To Jesus' right is the repentant criminal who in his final breath begged God for mercy and received it (looking upward); to Jesus' left is the unrepentant one who mocked God and found no mercy (looking downward). Behind them are his mother and Mary Magdalene,

---

3 Matthew 27:12-14.
4 Matthew 27:23.
5 Luke 23:39-43.

among the few followers who had not abandoned him after his betrayal the night before, now grieving in wonderment as he willingly faced crucifixion, an agonizing death where the body hangs for hours and ultimately dies from asphyxiation. The complete drama unfolds in four parallel accounts in Matthew 27, Mark 15, Luke 23 and John 18-19, with unique perspectives from each eyewitness.

Who would willingly endure such tragedy, and why wouldn't Jesus save himself? We look to the apex of the window for the mystery unveiled: the crucified Christ now comes forth from his tomb, gloriously resurrected, as evidenced by his nail-pierced hands, flanked by angels. Why should this surprise us? Hadn't Jesus on multiple occasions foretold his coming death and resurrection to his disciples, and hadn't they repeatedly dismissed his words as nonsense? As depicted by the red and white nimbi outlining his head in each scene, Jesus was God's Anointed for this very purpose.

By voluntarily offering himself as a sacrifice, Jesus took our judgment upon himself. And by visibly rising from the dead, Jesus demonstrated not only his power over death but also the truth of his claims. As John the Baptist had announced three years earlier, Jesus is the perfect Lamb of God who was sent to take away the sin of the world; he did so by redeeming (buying back) his people from all their sins dating back to the Garden of Eden, and counting them as his own. Today we can stand guiltless before God, washed in the blood of the Lamb, as if we had never sinned. The Resurrection is best understood by reading all four complementary accounts in Matthew 28, Mark 16, Luke 24 and John 20.

No, the dramatic sequence of events that we have come to label as "Holy Week" is nothing short of the culmination of Jesus' grand plan for his treasured people. Jesus would not save himself, for it was the only way to save *us*! It was "for the joy that was set before him that he endured the cross, despising the shame, and is seated at the right hand of the throne of God."[6] Far from events spiraling out of control, Holy Week was the deliberate working out of his heavenly plan, which Jesus had set in motion before the foundation of the world.

---

6   Jeremiah 31:3b and Hebrews 12:2.

Father, the hour has come ... I glorified thee on earth, having accomplished the work which thou gavest me to do; and now, Father, glorify thou me in thy own presence with the glory which I had with thee before the world was made.[7]

I am the resurrection and the life; he who believes in me, though he die, yet shall he live, and whoever lives and believes in me shall never die.[8]

The Story of the Family

Lewis Franklin Ellis, born November 1, 1907, was a St. Paul's communicant, lifelong attorney and president of Milligan-Reynolds Guaranty Title Agency. To this day the company occupies the same location at 724 Cherry St. as when it first opened in 1938. Mr. Ellis once served as president of the Tennessee Land Title Association, a statewide organization. A resident of Lookout Mountain, he died on December 2, 1992.

Katie Brown Ellis, his wife, was born on October 12, 1904. Also a St. Paul's communicant, she died on December 8, 1997, and is buried with her husband at Greenwood Cemetery in Chattanooga's Eastdale section.

---

7   Excerpts from John 17:1-5.
8   John 11:25-26.

The Stained Glass of St. Paul's

Design: *Chapel Studios, London, 1983*

8. APSE CORRIDOR

NELSON WINDOW

Why Are Some of Jesus' Teachings So Hard to Accept?

Is it mainly our modern minds and ears that wrestle with Jesus' miracles and teachings? Or did Jesus' ancient contemporaries also struggle to grasp what he was doing and saying—friend and foe alike? Without question, Jesus intentionally turned social norms upside down. He meant to grab their (and our) attention. He especially meant to confuse naysayers and doubters.

Jesus meant to jolt us awake from the routine of everyday life with scenarios/teachings/actions/etc. so extraordinary, and at times so offensive, to cause us pay attention and explore his teaching more deeply than we might otherwise. Much like an "X" marking the spot of buried treasure, Jesus' most confusing teachings/actions often mark the most profound implications of the Christian life that we must work to uncover and understand.

The Nelson window depicts two such miracles and parables that tug at our sensitivities, yet with a purpose: "[T]hese are written that you may believe that Jesus is the Christ, the Son of God, and that believing you may have life in his name."[1] Colored in red, buff, blue, purple, green, flesh, gray, magenta, orange and brown, the window was given in memory of Courtenay Quentin Nelson by his wife, Martha Nelson Godfrey, a St. Paul's communicant. It is one of four in the apse corridor behind the nave designed by Chapel Studios, London, and dedicated on Whitsunday, the Day of Pentecost, May 22, 1983. The window exhorts us not to give up so easily when one of Jesus' teachings or a particular Bible passage appears confusing or "contradictory". These have been included on purpose.

---

1 John 20:31.

The Story in the Window

"For my thoughts are not your thoughts, neither are your ways my ways, says the Lord."[2] Let's explore some of the ways Jesus turns our expectations of Him on its head.

In the lower right scene is depicted Jesus' miraculous restoration of the daughter of Jairus, the Roman centurion, shown lying on her deathbed. The reader will remember that, on the way to heal the girl, Jesus was detained by a woman tugging at his cloak. She had been ill for years, and her need was by no means an emergency. The disciples were annoyed, but Jesus had compassion and stopped. In the ensuing time in which Jesus lovingly conversed with the woman after healing her, word came from the centurion's home "not to bother the Teacher any more, for the girl is dead." Jesus responded, "Do not doubt, but believe." He continued on to Jairus' house, where he put out the mourners, took the dead girl by the hand, and restored her to life. The fact that he stopped along the way for a comparatively trivial need makes his miracle that much more impressive. *Incredible!*

The lower left scene is taken from Jesus' parable of the Good Samaritan, seen applying a bottle of oil to the wounds of a man beaten and left for dead by robbers. In the background a priest and Levite are seen passing by seemingly unbothered without helping the dying victim (Luke 10). Jesus' listeners would have been shocked: Would Israel's respectable clergy walk on by, while the most despised minority—the hated Samaritan—would stop to help? *Inconceivable!*

In the upper right scene we see Jesus' miraculous feeding of the 5,000, taken from Matthew 14, Mark 6, Luke 9 and John 6. As Jesus taught from a mountainside, people gathered from across the region to hear him. The day grew late, and soon the disciples began to worry that the people wouldn't make it home before dark. "Send them home so that they can get something to eat," the disciples told him. "You feed them," was Jesus' curt reply. The disciples were incredulous. All they had was a boy's basket of five loaves and two fishes; what good would that do? Jesus took the loaves and the fishes, gave thanks to God, and ordered it to be distributed. With each loaf or fish that was handed out, more

---

[2] Isaiah 55:8.

appeared in the baskets. After everyone was fed, 12 baskets full of leftover pieces were collected. *Impossible!*

The upper left-hand scene retells Jesus' parable of the Sower (Luke 8), who scatters seed on four kinds of ground from a basket in his hand, as the life-giving sun shines above. Some seed falls on tilled rows of good earth, some are devoured by birds on the path, some are choked by (green) thorns, and others are scorched along the rocky ground. It is God who allows his miracles and teachings to take root in the minds of some (good soil) and not others (the path, thorns and rocky ground). *Unconscionable!*

The Story of the Family

Courtenay Quentin Nelson was a prominent Chattanooga securities dealer who had been known to bring his office to his out-of-town customers by way of a 26½-foot Dodge motor home. A native of St. Paul, Minn., he was born on April 8, 1910, moved to Chattanooga in 1947 and joined the firm of Elder & Co. Four years later he and H.L. Thatcher organized Investment Securities Corp. with offices in the Read House. At St. Paul's he served as a vestryman, junior warden and president of the Layman's Service League. He also held the positions of secretary and trustee of the Episcopal Endowment Corp. for the former Diocese of Tennessee. Mr. Nelson served in the U.S. Navy in World War II, later retiring as a Reserve commander. He died on October 23, 1972, and is buried at the Chattanooga National Cemetery. In addition to his wife, he left his mother, Mrs. Axel Jonson, of Sioux Falls, S.D.; two daughters, Patricia and Barbara; and a sister, Mrs. Preston Scott, of Hecla, S.D.

Martha Lee Nelson Godfrey, who was born on May 30, 1911, outlived Mr. Nelson and her second husband, Leland B. Godfrey. A longtime communicant of St. Paul's, she was active in the Altar Guild and the Women of the Church. For 20 years she was chairman of candy stripers at Erlanger Medical Center. She was also past president of the Hospital Auxiliary, the first state coordinator of Hospital Auxiliaries, and southern regional chairwoman of the Committee on Hospital Auxiliaries for the American Hospital Association. By her death on December 22, 1990, she had five grandsons.

The Stained Glass of St. Paul's

Design: Chapel Studios, London, 1983

8. Apse Corridor

Lasley Window

Was Jesus God or Man?

We might wonder why, if Jesus really were God, he didn't experience a nobler birth. Or why he should experience childhood. Or, for that matter, why he should suffer death, much less a humiliating public execution. Why not enter the world as a full-grown man, get right to his mission and be crowned in glory at the end?

Perhaps his divine mission involved living as one of us, walking in our shoes so that he could legitimately atone for human sins by taking our place on a cross. Hebrews 2:17-18 tells us this was Jesus' plan all along.

But could he be divine and human at the same time? We learn most about someone by going back to his roots, to his earliest days. The Lasley window in the apse corridor running behind the high altar and outside the nave depicts four major events leading up to Jesus' ministry. Perhaps these four scenes, arranged chronologically from top to bottom, might shed light on Jesus' divine or human nature.

The window, along with three others in the apse corridor behind the nave, was designed by Chapel Studios, London, and dedicated on Whitsunday, the Day of Pentecost, May 22, 1983. It was given by Mr. and Mrs. John Edward O'Dell III in memory of her parents, Marshall M. Lasley and Augusta Allison Lasley. Very modern in style, reminiscent of a patchwork quilt, the window makes use of light tinted glass in subtle tones to maximize the gentle light source, and is colored in brown, tan, purple, green, red, orange, yellow, blue, white, gray and magenta.

The Story in the Window

Jesus' birth was nothing short of miraculous: foretold by prophets, announced by angels and born to a virgin. Certainly no mere mortal could orchestrate such circumstances. The topmost scene in this window depicts Luke 1:26-38, in what is known as the Annunciation. Here the angel Gabriel announces to the Virgin Mary that she is to be the mother of the long-awaited Messiah: "And behold, you will conceive in your womb and bear a son, and you shall call his name Jesus." The angel's instructions to Mary would have been significant, for Jesus' name means "God saves," indicating that Mary's son would be the one whom God would sacrifice in our place so that our sins might be forgiven.[1] "How can this be, since I have no husband?" Mary asked. The angel replied, "The Holy Spirit will come upon you, and the power of the Most High will overshadow you; therefore the child to be born will be called holy, the Son of God."

So while we normally think of a descending dove with three-rayed nimbus as symbolic of the Holy Spirit's appearance at Jesus' baptism[2], we remember that the Spirit also played a pivotal role in the Annunciation's aftermath. It's appropriate then that we see a dove in this scene swooping down toward Mary on the heels of Gabriel's message. In the arch of the window is a large lily, a standard symbol for the Annunciation. The event is observed on the church calendar on March 25.

Nine months later Jesus was born, and we see his Nativity depicted in the middle left scene, taken from Luke 2:1-7. What lowly conditions Jesus endured at his birth as he shared a cattle stall with barn animals, and what a particularly harsh ordeal this must have been for his mother. And yet, as we are reminded in hymn no. 78, "O Little Town

---

1 Matthew 1:21.
2 Mark 1:10-13.

of Bethlehem," through the gift of Jesus, "God imparts to human hearts the blessings of his heaven."[3]

Jews everywhere were returning to their ancestral towns to be counted in the Roman census. So it was that Joseph, a carpenter from Nazareth and a descendant of King David, traveled with his expectant bride to Bethlehem, the city of David. "While they were there, the time came for her to be delivered. And she gave birth to her first-born son and wrapped him in swaddling clothes, and laid him in a manger, because there was no place for them in the inn." Jesus' miraculous birth to a virgin is symbolically underscored as we see Mary in this scene, but not Joseph. Centuries earlier Isaiah had already prophesied that Jesus would be born of a virgin.[4]

As Jesus grew into adolescence, he amazed Israel's elders with an intellect that rivaled theirs.[5] Imagine a young boy of 12 in St. Paul's own Confirmation Class instructing seminary-trained clergy in the great truths of the Christian faith! Such was the strange sight that day in the temple at Jerusalem, and the people were astonished to hear him. The lower right-hand scene in this window beautifully captures this paradox, depicting the wise, old teachers of the law (notice them holding a scroll) seated attentively as the boy Jesus, shown in a red cross nimbus, lectures over them. Despite his extraordinary wisdom, Jesus walked in humility and submission to their authority even to the end.

As God, Jesus could have ministered alone quite easily, drawing from his infinite wisdom, riches and power. But Jesus, "though he was in the form of God, did not count equality with God a thing to be grasped, but emptied himself, taking the form of a servant, being born in the likeness of men. And being found in human form he humbled himself and became obedient unto death, even death on a cross."[6] "By his obedience, even to suffering and death, Jesus made the offering which we could not make; in him we are freed from the

---

3   "O Little Town of Bethlehem" 1982 Hymnal, no. 78.
4   Isaiah 7:14.
5   Luke 2:41-52.
6   Philippians 2:6-8.

power of sin and reconciled to God."[7] Only as a man could he suffer the cross in our place. Only as God could he rise again from the dead. He proved himself both!

In the bottom left-hand scene we see the Lord Jesus calling his first disciples, the two brothers Peter and Andrew, who were fisherman by the Sea of Galilee (taken from Matthew 4:18-20; Mark 1:16-18; Luke 5:1-11). "And he said to them, 'Follow me, and I will make you fishers of men.' Immediately they left their nets and followed him." When we take on the name "Christian," Jesus demands the same of his followers 2,000 years later. Have we dropped our personal ambitions (fishnets) in order to follow him? Though Jesus may not be physically standing over us as he is in this scene, he calls to us from his word and his Spirit just the same.

The Story of the Family

Marshall M. Lasley was president of Southern Clay Manufacturing Co. in Chattanooga, a business organized by his father as the Tennessee Paving Brick Co. In the days before macadam roads when most U.S. city streets were brick, it was reported that, "All the Chattanooga streets that [were] paved with brick, except Seventh street, were paved with the product of the company." Born in Chattanooga on November 6, 1893, to William Montague Lasley and Adele Marshall Lasley, he became a decorated Army captain in World War I. Mr. Lasley died on October 5, 1961.

Augusta Allison Lasley, his wife, with her husband raised a daughter, Elaine, who became Mrs. John E. O'Dell III, of Lookout Mountain. The Lasleys had five grandchildren. Mrs. Lasley died in October 1978, and was buried beside her husband at Forest Hills Cemetery, St. Elmo.

Elaine Lasley O'Dell, a lifelong Lookout Mountain resident, was an active communicant of St. Paul's, serving as both Sunday school teacher and Eucharistic lay minister. A Bright School graduate, she attended Ashley Hall in Charleston, S.C., graduated from Rosemary Hall in Baltimore, Md., and later attended the University

---

7 *Book of Common Prayer*, 850.

of Chattanooga. She was active for four decades in the U.S. Tennis Association as the National Women's and Men's Ranking Chairman as well as the National Juniors Ranking Chairman for girls 16's and 18's. She served 16 years on the board of directors for the Chattanooga Tennis Foundation, acting as president from 2009 to 2011. By the time of her death on November 19, 2013, she had nine grandchildren and two great-grandchildren. She is buried at Forest Hills Cemetery.

John Edward O'Dell III was a long-time area resident and St. Paul's communicant with a history in banking and real estate. Born on Christmas Day 1927 in Bristol, Tenn., to Assistant State Attorney General John E. O'Dell, Jr., and his wife, Frances Minton O'Dell, he was educated at Duncan Preparatory School and King College before serving in the U.S. Navy. Mr. O'Dell later founded and managed Shamrock Farms in Thomasville, Ga. He and his wife had several children: John Lasley O'Dell, Lauren O'Dell Ling, Anne O'Dell Faulk, Charlotte "Betsy" Scanlon and Katherine O'Dell Bailey. He died on August 1, 2000, and is buried at Blountville Cemetery in Sullivan County, Tennessee.

Design: Chapel Studios, London, 1983

8. APSE CORRIDOR

RAY WINDOW

How Did We Get Here, and Why Do We Suffer?

The Bible faces life's hard questions with unflinching directness. The Ray window addresses two of our weightiest of questions by depicting key scenes from the Old Testament: How did we get here, and why do we suffer? The window was given by Jack and Betty Ray, St. Paul's communicants, in memory of their mothers, Frances McMullan Ray (1896-1974) and Bertie May Camp Shelton (1893-1980). It was designed by Chapel Studios, London, and dedicated on the Day of Pentecost, Whitsunday, May 22, 1983. Like its neighboring windows in the apse corridor behind the nave, the Ray window is modern in style, reminiscent of a patchwork quilt, with use of light tinted glass in subtle tones to maximize the gentle light source. Its colors are green, blue, tan, brown, yellow, red and white.

The Story in the Window

> *"In the beginning God created the heavens and the earth. The earth was without form and void, and darkness was upon the face of the deep; and the Spirit of God was moving over the face of the waters."*[1]

---
1 Genesis 1:1-2.

So states the Bible's opening verse, summarizing how world history began. The upper left scene in this window depicts the first five days of creation, taken from Genesis 1. On the first day God created light. On the second day he created the sky, followed by land and vegetation on the third day, the sun and moon and stars on the fourth, creatures of the sea and air on the fifth and land animals and humans on the sixth. Finally, on the seventh day God rested. While scholars may disagree over how long the creation might have taken (six days or six eons?), we are content in recognizing that it was a definite chain of events, carried out by the active hand of God.

Up to this point everything that God had made was "very good". In the upper right scene is the lush Garden of Eden, over which God placed a man and woman to cultivate, each one bearing his image. They walked and talked with their heavenly Father, enjoyed food, fellowship and fruitful work. They had free roam of their earthly paradise, with one exception: "You may freely eat of every tree of the garden; but of the tree of the knowledge of good and evil you shall not eat, for in the day that you eat of it you shall die."[2] The Creator hardly sought fellowship with mindless robots, but he gave his human creatures the breath of life and the freedom to walk with him. After an initial season of intimacy with their Creator, our first parents are faced with a choice, taken from Genesis 3. Here we see Satan in the form of a serpent coiled in the branches of the tree of knowledge, sowing seeds of doubt in Eve's mind with a misleading question: "Did God say, 'You shall not eat of any tree of the garden'?"[3] Adam, spellbound by the serpent's suggestion that he could "be like God," joined his wife in eating the forbidden fruit, in direct disobedience to God. Immediately the eyes of both were opened, and the first couple begin enduring the painful consequences of broken fellowship with God and each other: shame, suffering and death. Our first parents tried hiding but were driven from the garden. God allowed them to experience the consequences of doing things their way.

God was patient with his creatures as they did not perish immediately but lived hundreds of years. But their wayward disobedience reached a tipping point by the time of the Great Flood (Genesis 6-9):

---

2 Genesis 2:16-17.
3 Genesis 3:1b.

> *The Lord saw that the wickedness of man was great in the earth, and that every imagination of the thoughts of his heart was only evil continually. And the Lord was sorry that he had made man on the earth, and it grieved him to his heart.*[4]

In the lower left scene we see how God acted to cleanse the earth with a cataclysmic flood. All perished except for one chosen servant, Noah, and his family. After months afloat inside a wooden ark, first during torrential rains and now as the waters recede, Noah sets free a succession of birds to determine whether it's safe to step outside the ark. As each bird returns, he is given a clue as to the water level. The first sign of life is when the dove returns with an olive branch (ancient symbol of peace), indicating that the Lord's wrath has subsided and deliverance is at hand. He will soon step onto dry land. Noah and his family are now given a command echoing the one given to Adam and Eve generations earlier: "And you, be fruitful and multiply, bring forth abundantly on the earth and multiply in it."[5]

Generations later, the real fruit of our first parents' disobedience lives on in their descendants: greed, violence, selfishness, injustice, pride, deceit, theft, abuse, discrimination, favoritism, extortion, bribery, murder. Is any of this how God originally designed his perfect creation to operate? Yet who among us is not guilty?

> *None is righteous, no not one; no one understands, no one seeks for God. All have turned aside, together they have gone wrong; no one does good, not even one. Their throat is an open grave, they use their tongues to deceive. The venom of asps (i.e. Satan, the serpent) is under their lips. Their mouth is full of curses and bitterness. Their feet are swift to shed blood, in their paths are ruin and misery, and the way of peace they do not know. There is no fear of God before their eyes.*[6]

> *Who can say, 'I have made my heart clean; I am pure from my sin'?*[7]

---

[4] Genesis 6:5-6.
[5] Genesis 9:7; Adam receives similar instructions in Genesis 1:28.
[6] Romans 3:10-18.
[7] Proverbs 20:9.

> *If we say we have no sin, we deceive ourselves, and the truth is not in us.*[8]

To help us confront our fallen human nature, God in his goodness gave us Ten Commandments, as a mirror into our souls. How else could we recognize our shortcomings than by facing God's perfect standard of righteousness, and our inability to keep it? As St. James said, "For whoever keeps the whole law but fails in one point has become guilty of all of it."[9] In the lower right scene, we see Moses, who personified the Ten Commandments, taken from Exodus 2. Born in a day when the Hebrews were cruelly enslaved by the Egyptians, Pharaoh had ordered their babies killed at birth to keep the demoralized people enslaved. Moses' mother hid her newborn inside a basket of bulrushes among the reeds of the Nile River. The baby was discovered providentially by the handmaidens of Pharaoh's daughter, who raised Moses as her own. As we imagine the joy on the princess' face at finding a baby for herself, we pause to reflect on Moses' birth mother's grief at giving up her baby to spare his life. Yet this sequence of events set in motion God's compassionate plan to deliver his people from their sufferings in Egypt.

A similar birth took place 1,500 years later in the New Testament, in which another wicked king sought to destroy every newborn, yet God spared one of them to deliver his people still suffering the curse of Adam and Eve. God has compassion on his suffering creatures, in spite of their waywardness disobedience. For he came to earth and "humbled himself to share our humanity."[10] Jesus endured every kind of suffering: poverty, loneliness, hunger, betrayal, beatings, injustice and execution, even rejection by his own Father, so that all who believe in him might be forgiven of their inherited disobedience and made right with God once again.[11] Through the gift of Jesus Christ, we can be assured that the answer to the hymnist's question in no. 140, "Wilt thou forgive those through which I run, and do run still, though still I do deplore?"[12] is a resounding "yes"!

---

8 1 John 1:8.
9 James 2:10.
10 *The Book of Common Prayer*, page 200.
11 Isaiah 53.
12 "Wilt Though Forgive That Sin, by Man Begun" *1982 Hymnal,* no. 140.

The Story of the Family

Dr. Charles "Jack" Jackson Ray was a St. Paul's vestryman and layreader and a proctologist in Chattanooga. Born in 1920, he moved here with his family in 1955 from New Orleans, where he had trained at the Ochsner Clinic under its founder, Dr. Alton Ochsner, and later served as chief of surgery at Charity Hospital in Bogalusa, La. He had a lifelong love of boating and deep-sea fishing and was at one time commodore of the Chattanooga Yacht Club. He retired from private practice in 1987 and, eight years later, returned to Louisiana, where he died in 2001.

Betty Shelton Ray, his wife, was a long-time Chattanooga yoga instructor. Born in 1922, she and her husband had three children: Brooke Arthurs and Becky Roninger, both of Louisiana, and Jack Ray of Minneapolis. Mrs. Ray died in 1999, and she is buried with her husband in their retirement hometown of Covington, La.

Bertie May Camp Shelton, Mrs. Ray's mother (August 6, 1893-August 1980), was married in 1918 to William "Jack" Shelton (November 17, 1887-September 11, 1946), a general agent in the Farm Credit Administration in Houston, Texas, and a U.S. Army intelligence officer during World War I. Both are buried at Greenleaf Cemetery in Brownwood, Texas.

Frances McMullan Ray, Dr. Ray's mother, was 78 years old when she died in December 1974. Born October 14, 1894, she was widow of Winston Jackson Ray and a member of First Christian Church. Mrs. Ray had lived with her son for the last eight years of her life at 1502 Lyndhurst Drive in Riverview. At the time of her death, she also left two sisters, Mrs. Beatty Wheddon of Dothan, Ala., and Mrs. Leonard Thomas of Montgomery, Ala. She is buried in Greenville, Ala.

Design: J. & R. Lamb Studios of New York, 1924

8. APSE CORRIDOR

NOLL WINDOW

Why Do Bad Things Happen to Good People?

Do you ever wonder why God allows evil and suffering? Strange as it may seem, many times it's so that good can prosper. The Bible is full of stories where God turned the wickedness done to one person into deliverance for many. We think of Joseph's brothers selling him into slavery, only to have him lead Egypt and the world out of famine. We remember how Job lost everything he had, and yet the record of his sufferings has brought comfort to untold millions. In the Noll window we see yet another example of bad things happening to good people so that others might prosper: the stoning of St. Stephen, taken from Acts 7:54-8:3. Stephen's murder launched a great persecution against the early church in Jerusalem, which scattered believers throughout the surrounding country. Through persecution the Gospel was spread farther and more rapidly, proving Tertullian's observation that "the blood of Christians is the seed of the church." Had this gruesome event never occurred, would the church have grown into a family of many nationalities and races that is today?

Found in the apse corridor in the back of the church, the Noll window is one of four depicting episodes in the life of St. Paul. Installed by J. & R. Lamb Studios of New York and dedicated on Pentecost Sunday,

June 8, 1924, the window is a memorial to Frederick Adams Noll (1876-1923), a lifelong communicant of St. Paul's. It was erected by his mother, Mary A. Schneider Noll. For many years this window was located in the east wall of the front vestibule of the church, where a door now leads to the cloister garden. Later it was moved to the south wall of the Strang Chapter Room at the base of the bell tower until its present relocation in 2002. The window is mounted in a wooden case on an interior wall and is, therefore, the only stained glass window in the church not illuminated by natural light. The Noll window is a good example of the layered glass technique. Pastel colors of salmon, purple, green, blue, yellow and pearl are predominant.

The Story in the Window

In this window we are witnessing Saul of Tarsus presiding over the stoning of St. Stephen, the church's first elected deacon and a fearless evangelist. It was this grisly yet glorious scene that made Stephen the first Christian martyr, whose "faith ne'er altered, nope ne'er faltered [because] the love Jesus filled [his] heart," as the hymn reminds us.[1]

The meaning of St. Stephen's execution is brought into sharper focus through an understanding of the events that prompted it, which are found in Acts 6 and 7. In the year or two immediately following Jesus' crucifixion and resurrection, the church quickly grew from a small band of disciples to a family of thousands. This is certainly not what the religious leaders of Judah had hoped for by "eliminating" Jesus, their enemy. So, just as they had done to Jesus, they trumped up false charges against Stephen, a particularly outspoken church leader. Brought before the ruling council, or Sanhedrin, Stephen delivered a powerful summary of the Old Testament, concluding: God has loved you like a father, but you have killed all his messengers. "But they cried out with a loud voice and stopped their ears and rushed together upon him. Then they cast him out of the city and stoned him; and the witnesses laid down their garments at the feet of a young man named Saul."

---

[1] "Blessed feasts of blessed martyrs" 1982 Hymnal, no. 238.

In the upper left appearing in a simple circle nimbus, we see St. Stephen in prayer. Scripture tells us that he was asking God to forgive his attackers. What marvelous faith and mercy this is! Christians continue to be inspired by "the example of the first martyr Stephen, who looked up to heaven and prayed for his persecutors."[2] Yet how hard it is for any of us to forgive small injustices against ourselves—a driver cutting us off on the roadway, for example—much less a violent mob bent on destroying us with phony evidence and large rocks. As we observe the walls of Jerusalem at the peak of the window's arch, we are reminded of Jesus' ominous lament: "O Jerusalem, Jerusalem, killing the prophets and stoning those who are sent to you! How often would I have gathered your children together as a hen gathers her brood under her wings, and you would not!"[3] The inscription from Acts 8:1 near the bottom of the window succinctly sums up the scene: "And Saul was consenting unto Stephen's death." Jewish law provided that an accuser would cast the first stone at the convicted criminal's execution. So in protecting the garments of these false witnesses, Saul is clearly a conspirator in Stephen's undoing, perhaps having coached their testimony.

Here is the Bible's first mention of Saul, a supremely well-educated man who became a visible leader in the persecution of the early church. In fact, the Bible says that Saul "laid waste the church, and entering house after house, he dragged off men and women and committed them to prison." It is significant that Saul here wears a red cloak, a color that is symbolic of many things, including hate. The original placement of this window in 1924 outside the nave was done deliberately to symbolize that Saul himself was still outside the Church when these events took place. But here is the amazing power and boundless mercy of God, who alone can change the one who calls himself "the foremost of sinners"[4] into a righteous saint.

This same God has changed the lives of countless millions over the centuries, building for himself a global family that will reign with him at Christ's return. Have we been changed by God? Even if our

---

2 *The Book of Common Prayer*, page 186.
3 Matthew 23:37.
4 I Timothy 1:15.

conversion is not as dramatic as St. Paul's, do our own lives show evidence of being touched by God? Over time, has our desire for worldly things (possessions, power or popularity) diminished? Has our love for God and knowledge of His ways grown? Has our concern for the suffering and our compassion for others increased? If so, then God is at work changing our hearts from within and, as the old hymn says, we will "be in that number ... when the saints come marching in!"

The Story of the Family

Frederick Adams Noll was a devoted communicant and vestryman of St. Paul's and Chattanooga lawyer. Born in 1876 to Adam and Mary A. Noll, he was educated in the local public schools and graduated with high honors from Chattanooga High School in 1896. After obtaining his law degree at Columbia University, he returned to his hometown to form a practice with Nathan L. Bachman, who later became a justice of the Tennessee Supreme Court and U.S. Senator from Tennessee. In the subsequent years Mr. Noll formed various law partnerships with Robert B. Cooke, Sam J. McAllester, Thomas H. Cooke and W.B. Swaney. As a young attorney Mr. Noll was considered one of the brightest, most diligent lawyers at the Chattanooga bar. He also served as treasurer and a member of the board of directors of the Chattanooga Public Library, which at that time was located in the Carnegie Library building still standing at the southeast corner of Eighth Street and Georgia Avenue. He was also a faculty member at the Chattanooga College of Law and served a term as treasurer of the St. Paul's vestry in 1903. He was married at St. Paul's on April 10, 1912, to Miss Christine Norcross of Cincinnati. Mr. Noll died on October 16, 1923, at his home on 860 Vine St., following a yearlong illness that forced him to abandon his law practice in the final month of his life. He is buried at Forest Hills Cemetery, St. Elmo.

Mary A. Schneider Noll, his mother, was born about 1852 to Frederick Phillip Schneider and Maria Hockenettle Schneider, immigrants from Germany and France, respectively. Her father, who came to Chattanooga around 1851, was one of the city's pioneer downtown merchants, an expert cabinetmaker and photographer, who lived with his family on the side of Cameron Hill. In 1873, Mary married Adam Noll. She had two other sons at the time of Frederick's death, Louis M. Noll of Tyner and William L. Noll of Montgomery, Ala. She died on March 7, 1942, and is buried near her son.

Adam Noll, her husband, was born on March 28, 1836, in Dusseldorf, Germany. He operated a grocery in the three-story brick Noll Building at 707 Market St. that was so sturdy it helped to stop the spread of a raging fire in downtown Chattanooga on Nov. 10, 1871. Located next door to the present-day First Tennessee Bank, the Noll Building was torn down in the 1960s. Mr. Noll died on March 24, 1885, and is buried beside his wife.

The Stained Glass of St. Paul's

Design: Heaton, Butler and Bayne, London, 1925

9. NAVE

ANDREWS WINDOW

What Must I Do to Know God?

A Pharisee named Nicodemus came to see Jesus late one night with a pressing question. Anticipating Nicodemus' question before it was even asked, Jesus answered, "Truly, truly I say to you, unless one is born anew, he cannot see the kingdom of God." The dialogue that follows in John 3 may be the most enigmatic conversation recorded in the Bible. Jesus' response reveals the question which Nicodemus had in mind: What must I do to know God? The Andrews window, the tall lancet above the front entrance to the church, illumines the great mystery of spiritual rebirth, explaining what Jesus meant by saying "born anew" or, in the words of the old King James Version, "born again".

Made by the London studio of Heaton, Butler & Bayne, this Gothic-style window originated partly in response to the rector's (later Bishop John D. Wing of Florida) expressed hope to "beautify the church." For many years it was pictured on the cover of *Weekly Chimes*, the parish bulletin. Given by Mr. and Mrs. Garnett Andrews III in 1924 and installed in 1925, it is a memorial to his father Col. Garnett Andrews, C.S.A. (1837-1903), and the couple's deceased children Garnett Andrews IV (1900-04) and Margaret Avery Andrews (1907-17). It depicts the rebirth of Saul of Tarsus, a Jew and Pharisee, afterward called Paul, our parish's patron saint. His emblem, found near the bottom of the window just above the inscription, is a shield bearing a sword. Composed of stained and painted glass, this colorful window is a late example of the light effects in the finest Art Noveau stained glass. The artist has made superb use of the vertical space, drawing the beam of light down from the very top of the window and shining its rays on both Saul and the viewer. Arched Gothic traceries are set at the window's top and bottom. Its side borders are lined with stone gargoyles, whose dark shades contrast the bright colors of the glass—red, purple, yellow, gray, blue, flesh tone and brown. To really appreciate its great beauty, one should stand in either of two places: (1) directly in front of the high altar or (2) directly beneath the window on the ground floor of the nave.

The Story in the Window

In the years immediately following Jesus' death and crucifixion, St. Paul became the young church's fiercest enemy. Christians lived in terror of Saul, as he was called, who the Bible says would breathe out murderous threats. Saul was a conspirator in the stoning of St. Stephen, the first Christian martyr. In his zeal to stamp out this new Jewish sect, Saul harassed and threatened members of "The Way," even obtaining a formal commission along with a Roman military escort to jail believers for their faith.

On his way from Jerusalem to arrest Christians in Damascus, he was halted by a sudden flash of light from heaven. "Saul, Saul, why persecutest thou me?" reads the inscription near the bottom of the window. With these words from Acts 9:4, Saul was thrown to the ground and struck blind. "Who are you, Lord?" Saul responded, his arm shielding his face from the unbearable light as a Roman centurion holding a spear rushes to his aid. "I am Jesus, whom you are persecuting," boomed the voice from heaven. Saul's traveling companions stood speechless, hearing but seeing no one. The arrogant, self-righteous Saul was instantly humbled, shown here with his knees visually buckling under the crushing weight of the characters standing over him in the window's background. His armor lies strewn along the path.

When the voice had ceased, Saul lay blind and was led by the hand to Damascus, where he spent three days without eating or drinking, a man with "a contrite and humble spirit".[1] After the Lord restored Saul's sight three days later, he began preaching that Jesus is the Son of God. The Jews and Christians were equally incredulous. "Is this Saul?" Could the Church's greatest tormentor have turned into her greatest champion overnight?

No doubt the people had wondered the same thing about Jesus' disciples years earlier. What caused Peter, who feared for his life, to cowardly deny Christ one day and boldly proclaim him the next? What made the disillusioned band of fishermen and tax collectors who had barricaded themselves in the upper room after Jesus' crucifixion suddenly take to the streets with a public proclamation that would surely result in death or imprisonment: "Repent, for the kingdom of God is at hand!"[2] In each case, their hearts were humbled and their eyes were open to who Jesus is: the living God whose "love so amazing, so divine, demands my soul, my life, my all."[3] Those who truly love Jesus have undergone a similar inward transformation. Their outward circumstances may not played out as dramatically as St. Paul's blinding, yet it was no less miraculous. "Having his wonderful conversion in mind," may we "show ourselves thankful to [God] by following his holy teaching, through Christ Jesus our Lord."[4]

The Story of the Family

Col. Garnett Andrews, a prominent Chattanooga lawyer after the War Between the States, was born in Wilkes County, Ga., on May 15, 1837, to Judge Garnett Andrews and Annulet Ball Andrews. He graduated from the University of Georgia and admitted to the bar in 1859. He was the first man in his county to enter the Confederate army, in 1861. With a distinguished war record as artillery officer and judge advocate, he was severely wounded, most

---
1 Isaiah 57:15.
2 Matthew 3:2.
3 "When I Survey the Wondrous Cross," *1982 Hymnal*, no. 474.
4 *Book of Common Prayer*, 238-239.

critically in a skirmish at Salisbury, N.C., three days after General Lee's surrender but survived. Col. Andrews married Miss Rosalie Champe Beirne of Monroe County, Va., in 1867, fathering seven children. Before coming to Chattanooga in 1881, he practiced law and edited a newspaper in Yazoo City, Miss. He served as Chattanooga's mayor from 1891 to 1893, a St. Paul's vestryman from 1884 until his death, a Mason and a Knight of Pythias. He died May 16, 1903. He and his wife are buried at Resthaven Cemetery in Washington, Ga.

Garnett Andrews III, the colonel's son, was a St. Paul's vestryman who in 1897 established Chattanooga's first textile mill. Richmond Hosiery Mills would become the city's largest private employer. Born in Wilkes County, Ga., on September 15, 1870, Mr. Andrews moved with his parents to Chattanooga as a boy and was educated here. He became a cadet at Virginia Military Institute and studied at Worcester Polytechnic Institute of Massachusetts. He married in 1895 the former Elizabeth Lenoir Key, daughter of Judge David McKendree Key and sister of Mrs. Z.C. Patten, who is memorialized in the Patten Light of the World window. From their home at 511 East Fourth St., near the present-day head of Veterans Bridge, they raised several children: Betty (Mrs. J. Berens Waters of New York), Katherine (Mrs. Samuel C. Hutchinson of Chattanooga), Garnett IV (in whose memory this window is given), Garnett Jr. (named for his deceased brother), David Key Andrews and Margaret Avery Andrews (also in whose memory this window is given). Mrs. Andrews died in August 26, 1936, at age 61, and her husband followed on November 11, 1946. Both are buried at Forest Hills Cemetery, St. Elmo.

Margaret Avery Andrews, known by her pet name "Miss Mag," was born in Chattanooga on January 25, 1907, to Mr. and Mrs. Garnett Andrews III. At age 10, on April 24, 1917, she wore a crepe paper costume to a children's fancy dress party at St. Paul's, as her mother helped in the old parish kitchen above the Ava Wright Room. The event was in aid to the Red Cross work at the beginning of America's involvement in World War I. Her costume caught fire by the stove, and she died of burns three weeks later on May 14. In her memory her parents established the Little Miss Mag Day Nursery, where St. Paul's communicant Jo Ann Albright served as director for many years. She is buried at Forest Hills Cemetery.

Garnett Andrews IV, born in 1900, was only 4 years old when he died of colitis and hepatitis on March 29, 1904. He is buried at Forest Hills Cemetery.

Garnett Andrews, Jr., was named for his deceased brother at his birth on November 15, 1905, the year following Garnett IV's death. The surviving son followed in his father's footsteps as a Chattanooga textile executive and St. Paul's vestryman, at one time also serving as junior warden. He became president of Richmond Sales Co. after first serving in executive roles in several hosiery companies in America and England, including Ballito Hosiery Mill, Arrowhead Fashion Mills and his father's mill in Chattanooga. Mr. Andrews was active on the boards of the Children's Home and the Pine Breeze Sanatorium, which at one time was perched atop Stringer's Ridge. He married Lillian Kitrell on June 12, 1935. He died on April 3, 1967, and she followed in October 1973. Both are buried at Forest Hills Cemetery, St. Elmo.

The Stained Glass of St. Paul's

Design: Chapel Studios, London, 1981

10. KEY-ANDREWS HALL VESTIBULE

KIDD BAPTISMAL WINDOW

Why Observe Baptism?

For 2,000 years, Christians of every kind have practiced the sacrament of Holy Baptism. What is the origin and meaning behind this public ritual washing? With its vibrant colors and memorable imagery, the Kidd window gives us a moving answer to this question. Designed as a companion to the adjacent Hailey Eucharist window, the Kidd Baptismal window is aglow with earth-tones of blue, green, orange, yellow, white, brown and gray. A rough white stone border adds depth and is reminiscent of the church building's exterior stone trim. While the window is predominantly blue, in the lower panels the warm, brick-like tones and architectural features clearly depict St. Paul's.

Situated on the south side of the front door in the Key-Andrews Hall vestibule, it was given in memory of young Robert Dobson Kidd (1957-71) by the J. Inman Kidd family, communicants of St. Paul's and dedicated on St. Thomas Day, December 21, 1981, to mark the 10th anniversary of his death. It was made by Chapel Studios in London.

The Story in the Window

Baptism has its root in the Old Testament practice of circumcision. In Genesis 17:11, God commanded his servant Abraham that every male in his household should be circumcised as a sign of their special relationship to Him. In the New Testament, this sign was fulfilled and replaced by water baptism. (We see the same principle at work in other Old Testament practices: the annual Passover was fulfilled and replaced with the Lord's Supper; daily animal sacrifices were fulfilled once and for all by Christ's self-sacrifice on the cross, etc.) Baptism is a ritual cleansing of sin,[1] an outward sign to symbolize the inward reality of a person set apart by God and for God and welcomed into the community of faith. As the *Book of Common Prayer* explains,

> *Holy Baptism is a full initiation by water and the Holy Spirit into Christ's Body the Church. The bond which God establishes in Baptism is indissoluble.*[2]

Elsewhere,

> *Baptism is not only a sign of profession, and mark of difference … but it is also a sign of Regeneration or New Birth.*[3]

There are two scenes in the window depicting two forms of baptism found in the New Testament. The upper scene shows Christ's baptism in the River Jordan by John the Baptist, found in Matthew 3, Mark 1, Luke 3 and John 1. A white dove in a gold cross nimbus is above Christ's head, symbolizing the descent from heaven by the Holy Spirit onto Jesus when a voice from above was heard saying, "This is my beloved Son, with whom I am well pleased." A group of onlookers are also pictured.

The lower scene shows a baptism being conducted nearly 2,000 years later at St. Paul's. With the bell tower, organ pipes and interior arches in the background, the baptismal font rests in the rear of the nave. Around it stands a priest—might he bear resemblance to Dr. John H. Bonner, St. Paul's young new rector when Robert was born, holding a baby attended by his parents and godparents? In the Episcopal Church, as in many other churches, we baptize infants just as the Israelites circumcised infants, a sign that they are dedicated to God and included in the family of God.

It is important to note that the sort of baptism practiced by John the Baptist is somewhat different. Unlike Christian baptism or Jewish

---

[1] Acts 22:16.
[2] *Book of Common Prayer*, 298.
[3] Articles of Religion, *Book of Common Prayer*, 873.

circumcision, John's baptism symbolized repentance—urging hearers to make way in their lives and their hearts for the long-awaited Messiah, the one appointed and empowered by God to forgive sins. Though similar in appearance to Christian baptism, the need for John's baptism ended with the beginning of Jesus' earthly ministry since the Kingdom of God had now finally arrived: "He (Jesus) must increase, but I (John) must decrease," the baptizer said to his followers.[4] Shortly afterward, he was beheaded.

The two events, though 2,000 years apart, are united through space and time in their significance: Neither baptism truly washed anyone in God's sight; they were outward signs representing the inner reality of what God's was doing on the inside.

The Story of the Family

Robert Dobson Kidd was 14 years old when he died in 1971. He lived at 425 Glenwood Drive near Memorial Hospital with his parents, J. Inman and Rebecca Love Kidd. He had a brother, Frank Inman Kidd, and two sisters: Jane Bagley, of Athens, Ga.; and Marian Riggar, of Chattanooga. He is buried in LaFayette, Ga.

J. Inman Kidd, his father, was a 52-year communicant of St. Paul's and a former president of Chattanooga Gas Co. A native of Hartwell, Ga., he graduated from Darlington School in Rome and later the University of Georgia. He was married to Rebecca Lee Love Kidd and was employed with Atlanta Gas Co. in 1941 before serving in World War II as a technical supply clerk in ground service for the 5th Air Force in New Guinea and the Philippines. After the war he worked as a CPA before being hired as an auditor for Chattanooga Gas Co. in 1952. He was steadily promoted over the years until he became president in 1974. He held that post until his retirement in 1989. He once served as president of the Chattanooga Chapter of the Tennessee Society of Certified Public Accountants and president of the Metropolitan Council of Community Services. At St. Paul's he served 11 years as treasurer, two years as senior warden, and for many years as a crucifer and acolyte at burial services. Mr. Kidd died on November 19, 2000, at the age of 80.

---

4   John 3:30.

The Stained Glass of St. Paul's

Design: Chapel Studios, London, 1981

10. Key-Andrews Hall Vestibule

HAILEY EUCHARIST WINDOW

Why Celebrate Communion?

If any regular feast unites believers around the world, it is the Holy Eucharist, or Last Supper. The Hailey window, designed as a companion to the adjacent Kidd Baptismal window in the Key-Andrews Hall vestibule, reminds us why we celebrate Christian Communion, which fulfilled and took the place of the Old Testament Passover feast. The window, imbued with earth tones of gold, red, green, purple and blue, is surrounded by a rough white stone border. This feature both adds depth and is reminiscent of the exterior trim of Key-Andrews Hall. Made by Chapel Studios of London, it was given in memory of Wilburn Cantrell Hailey (1896-1977) and Dorothy Clark Hailey (1899-1980) by the Hailey family, communicants of St. Paul's, and dedicated on Thanksgiving Day, 1981.

The Story in the Window

Jesus' remarkable three-year ministry had culminated in his triumphant entry into Jerusalem with shouts of "hosanna" from worshipers waving palms. After vehemently driving away the moneychangers from the temple and publicly silencing his haughty opponents with simple parables, Jesus was anointed by the sinful woman at Bethany for all to see. And now here were his twelve closest companions gathered around their Master for the Jewish Passover, the historic national feast, jockeying for positions of power in the great revolution they believed was about to occur. Their hour of national deliverance from the Roman yoke had come, and their long-awaited political savior was before them!

But Jesus had something else in mind entirely: "Little children, yet a little while I am with you … Where I am going you cannot come."[1] "I have earnestly desired to eat this Passover with you before I suffer."[2] "You will all fall away because of me this night."[3] "Truly, I say to you, one of you will betray me, one who is eating with me."[4]

We can only imagine how the disciples' giddy excitement turned to unsettling anxiety. What could Jesus possibly mean by suffering and betrayal? Where was he going, and why couldn't they join him? We enter now the portion of that scene that lives on each week in our order of the Holy Communion, specifically the Great Thanksgiving and the Breaking of the Bread. Jesus turned to his stone-faced followers with a picture of what was about to occur:

> *"Take, eat: This is my Body, which is given for you. Do this for the remembrance of me … Drink this, all of you: This is my Blood of the new Covenant, which is shed for you and for many for the forgiveness of sins."*[5]

Jesus knew he was the Passover Lamb foretold in Scripture: His body would be pierced, and his blood would be spilled as a sacrifice to God. For the revolutionaries among Jesus' disciples, was this really a victory? Yes! Not a political win over Rome, but a cosmic win over sin. Ever since Adam and Eve's fall, it has been our inherent sin which prompts men to act selfishly toward their neighbor; it is our inherent sin that leaves us unconcerned about our care for creation; it is sin that cools our affections toward God; it is sin that replaces the Great Commission in our hearts with other "priorities"; it is sin that will proclaim us guilty at the Judgment for violating God's perfect law— and this sin lives in every one of us. Just as animal sacrifices in the Old Testament "cleared" the Israelite of his guilt by taking his place, Jesus' sacrifice on the cross would clear his followers of their sin. As the Hymnist reminds us, in Christ's "death our sins are dead."[6]

---

1 John 13:33.
2 Luke 22:15.
3 Matthew 26:31.
4 Mark 14:18.
5 *Book of Common Prayer*, 362-3.
6 "Bread of the World in Mercy Broken," 1982 Hymnal no. 301.

The Hailey window depicts the events described in Matthew 26, Mark 14, Luke 22 and 1 Corinthians 11. It shows Christ giving thanks at the head of the table, his head outlined in a white-and-gold cross nimbus as he holds the wine in one hand and bread in the other. Yet it wasn't until after Jesus' resurrection and the Holy Spirit's arrival that the disciples understood the significance of the Last Supper. We are to "do this in remembrance" of not only him but also of what he was about to do—die in their (and our) place. The whole scene is framed by a symbolic border containing clusters of grapes, grapevines and golden ears of wheat—elements of the Last Supper. At the top of the window is an ornate gold chalice containing a white wafer, the traditional symbol for Holy Eucharist or Maundy Thursday, the day these events originally took place around the year 30 A.D.

The Story of the Family

Wilburn Cantrell Hailey was a Chevrolet dealer in Chattanooga for nearly 40 years. Born on May 5, 1896, to Myra Cantrell and Romans Hailey in Goodlettsville, Tenn., he was schooled in Pulaski and Nashville before enlisting in the Army. He served in the First World War in France and Germany before returning to Nashville and becoming general manager of Jim Reed Chevrolet Co. He moved to Signal Mountain in 1940 and bought Hamilton Motor Co., later known as Hailey Chevrolet. After selling that company to Ed Wright in 1971, he and his son, Wilburn, Jr., organized Hailey Porsche-Audi Co. Mr. Hailey was a past president of the Chattanooga Automobile Dealers Association and a longtime communicant of St. Paul's, where he served on the vestry. He also served as a Signal Mountain town commissioner. Mr. Hailey died July 9, 1977.

Dorothy Clark Hailey was the daughter of Ira B. and Katherine Lane Townes Clark and a Nashville native born in 1899. She was active in the Red Cross Auxiliary Ladies at Erlanger Hospital, the Colonial Dames and the Daughters of the American Revolution. Mrs. Hailey died on November 16, 1980, and is buried beside her husband at Forest Hills Cemetery, St. Elmo.

LIST OF BIOGRAPHICAL SKETCHES

Alexander, Thomas D. (1917-98)

Andrews, Col. Garnett (1837-1903)

Andrews, Garnett III (1870-1946)

Andrews, Garnett IV (1900-04)

Andrews, Garnett Jr. (1905-67)

Andrews, Margaret Avery (1907-17)

Brown, C. Victor (ca. 1862-1929)

Brown, Mattie Davidson (1865-94)

Carlile, Marion A. Bendring (1838-1926)

Carlile, Thomas J. (1833-78)

Chapman, Julia Bloomfield (1855-1900)

Davidson, Charles Alexander (1832-99)

Davidson, Edward (1871-1931)

Davidson, Margaret Jane Mowbray (1829-1911)

Ellis, Katie Brown (1904-97)

Ellis, Lewis Franklin (1907-92)

Garvin, Minnie Newman (1862-1918)

Garvin, Judge Walter Brown (ca. 1862-1934)

Godfrey, Martha Lee Nelson (1911-90)

Hailey, Dorothy Clark (1899-1980)

Hailey, Wilburn Cantrell (1896-1977)

Kidd, J. Inman (ca. 1920-2000)

Kidd, Robert Dobson (ca. 1957-71)

Lasley, Augusta Allison (-1978)

Lasley, Marshall M. (1893-1961)

Nelson, Courtenay Quentin (1910-72)

Nieland, Helen A. Carlile (ca. 1860-1932)

Noll, Adam (1836-85)

Noll, Frederick Adams (1876-1923)

Noll, Mary A. Schneider (ca. 1852-1942)

Nottingham, Annie Grace Rathburn (ca. 1867-1939)

O'Dell, Elaine Lasley (-2013)

O'Dell, John Edward III (1927-2000)

Overmyer, Donald Howard (1907-90)

Overmyer, Ruth Elberfeld (1910-94)

Patten, Elizabeth Nelson Bryan (1907-90)

Patten, Sarah Key (1864-1958)

Patten, Z.C. (1840-1925)

Patten, Z. Cartter Jr. (1903-82)

Rathburn, Catherine Whiton Daniel (-1910)

Rathburn, Nellie (ca. 1856-1872)

Rathburn, William Perry (1822-84)

Ray, Betty Shelton (1922-99)

Ray, Dr. Charles "Jack" Jackson (1920-2001)

Ray, Frances McMullan (1894-1974)

Record, Margaret Milne (-1983)

Record, Dr. W.D.L. (-1983)

Reeves, Frances M. Starrett (-1908)

Reeves, Dr. James Edmond (1829-96)

Shelton, Bertie May Camp (1893-1980)

Staley, Jennie Martha (1866-91)

Whiteside, Judge Hugh (1854-96)

BIBLIOGRAPHY

General
A 125th Birthday Celebration, *The Year of the Dandelion: St. Paul's Church, Stained Glass Windows* [1978].
The Book of Common Prayer (New York: The Church Hymnal Corp., 1979).
The Holy Bible: Revised Standard Version (New York: Thomas Nelson & Sons, 1952).
The Hymnal 1982 (New York: The Church Hymnal Corp., 1985).
Allen Chesney, "Stained Glass at St. Paul's" (Centennial Chimes, St. Paul's Episcopal Church, Chattanooga, Tenn., May 8, 1988).
Herbert W. Kaiser, "Stained Glass Windows of Saint Paul's Church" (1976).
Herbert W. Kaiser, "Windows Add Immeasurable Dimensions: Glory Shines in Stained Glass" (n.d.).
Edwin Lindsey, *Centennial History of St. Paul's Episcopal Church Chattanooga, Tennessee 1853-1953* (Chattanooga, Tenn.: Vestry of St. Paul's Parish, 1953).
Edwin Lindsey, *History of St. Paul's Episcopal Church Chattanooga, Tennessee 1953 to 1972* (Chattanooga, Tenn.: Vestry of St. Paul's Parish, 1972).
W. Ellwood Post, *Saints, Signs, and Symbols*, 2nd ed., with foreword by the Rev. Cannon Edward N. West (Wilton, Conn.: Morehouse-Barlow, 1980).
John K. Powell, *History of St. Paul's Church: With an Account of the Introduction of the Episcopal Church into TN* (Chattanooga, Tenn.: Morgan Print Co., 1923).
Mimi Steinberg and Sally L. Reeve-Smith, eds., *Cooking up Memories: A Celebration of Heavenly Recipes for the Pleasure of Your Table and History for Your Memories* (Chattanooga, Tenn.: St. Paul's Episcopal Church, 2000).
John Wilson, *Chattanooga's Story* (Chattanooga, Tenn.: Roy McDonald, 1980).

Alexander Parable Windows
"Dedication of the Clerestory Windows," Sunday bulletin insert, St. Paul's Episcopal Church, Chattanooga, Tenn., October 12, 1997.
Obituary of Thomas D. Alexander (*The Chattanooga Times*, August 20, 1998), B2.

Andrews Window
"Andrews, 61, Dies; Was Textile Man" (*The Chattanooga Times*, April 4, 1967).
"Death of 'Miss Mag' Early Yesterday Morning: Victim of Accident Succumbs to the Burns Sustained April 24" (*The Daily Times*, Chattanooga, Tenn., May 15, 1917).
Will T. Hale and Dixon L. Merritt, *A History of Tennessee and Tennesseans: The Leaders and Representative Men in Commerce, Industry and Modern Activities*, vol. 7 (Chicago and New York: The Lewis Publishing Co., 1913), 2144-7.
Mrs. Julian C. Lane, *Key and Allied Families* (Press of the J.W. Burke Co., 1931), 82-3, 86-7.

Chapman Window
"Funeral of Miss Julia Chapman" (*The Chattanooga Times*, February 19, 1900).
"Miss Josephine Chapman: Death of a Former Well Known Chattanooga Teacher" (*The Chattanooga Times*, May 15, 1911).
"Miss Chapman's Funeral: Fitting Honor to Be Paid to Her Memory This Afternoon" (*The Chattanooga Times*, May 16, 1911).
"Miss Chapman's Funeral: Impressive Services at St. Paul's and Forest Hills" (*The Chattanooga Times*, May 17, 1911).
William Nelson, *New Jersey Biographical and Genealogical Notes: from the Volumes of the New Jersey Archives, with Additions and Supplements* (Genealogical Publishing Com, 1916), 39.

Davidson-Brown Window
Cox, Steven. "Chattanooga Was His Town: The Life of General John T. Wilder" (*Chattanooga Regional Historical Quarterly*, 7.1, 2004) http://www.johnsonsdepot.com/tweetsie/wilder_scox.pdf

Cullon Hooks, Highland Park Historic Resources Survey, September 30, 2005, http://chattanooganeighborhood.com/HighlandParkSurvey_2005.pdf.

"Edward Davidson, 60, Merchant, Dies: Pioneer Clothing Man Victim of Long Illness: Active in Chattanooga Affairs for Forty Years—Funeral Set for Today" (*The Chattanooga Times*, November 6, 1931), 3.

"50 Years Ago …" (Hamilton County Herald, May 7, 2010).

"Gives a Memorial Window: Mr. and Mrs. Edward Davidson Present It to St. Paul's Church" (*The Daily Times*, Chattanooga, Tenn., August 5, 1916).

"A Sweet Life Ended: Mrs. C.V. Brown Passed Away This Morning," (*The Daily Times*, Chattanooga, Tenn., March 20, 1894), 2.

Ruth Robinson, "The Little Brown Church in the Wildwood," (The Chattanoogan, December 17, 2008). https://www.chattanoogan.com/2008/12/17/141004/The-Little-Brown-Church-In-The-Wildwood.aspx

Obituary of Mrs. C. Victor Brown (*The Chattanooga Times*, December 29, 1946).

Obituary of Victor C. Brown (*The Chattanooga Times*, November 24, 1929).

Ellis Window
Obituary of Katie B. Ellis (*The Chattanooga Times*, December 9, 1997).

Obituary of Lewis F. Ellis (*The Chattanooga Times*, December 3, 1992), A10.

Garvin St. George Window
"Death in Baltimore of Mrs. W.B. Garvin" (*The Daily Times*, Chattanooga, Tenn., January 24, 1918), 3.

Obituary of Walter Brown Garvin, (*The Chattanooga Times*, January 27, 1934).

Hailey Eucharist Window
Obituary of Mrs. Dorothy Clark Hailey (*The Chattanooga Times*, November 17, 1980), A4.

"History in Glass" (*The Chattanooga Times*, December 19, 1981), F1.

"W.C. Hailey, Car Dealer, Dead at 81" (*The Chattanooga Times*, July 10, 1977), A1, 8.

Kidd Baptismal Window
"History in Glass" (*The Chattanooga Times*, December 19, 1981), F-1.

Obituary of J. Inman Kidd (*Chattanooga Times Free Press*, November 20, 2000).

Obituary of Robert Dobson Kidd (*The Chattanooga Times*, December 22, 1971), 2.

Lasley Window
"Lasley Is Dead; Manufacturer: Illness Forced Retirement of Veteran, 68—from Prominent Family" (*The Chattanooga Times*, October 6, 1961), 11.

Obituary of Mrs. Augusta Allison Lasley (*The Chattanooga Times*, October 12, 1978), C5.

Bureau of Labor Statistics and Mines of the State of Tennessee, *Second Annual Report of the Commissioner of Labor and Inspector of Mines, To His Excellency, Governor John P. Buchanan, 1892* (Nashville: Marshall & Bruce, 1893), 117.

Obituary of Elaine Lasley O'Dell (*Chattanooga Times Free Press*, November 21, 2013).

Obituary of John O'Dell III (*The Chattanooga Times*, August 3, 2000), B4.

Nelson Window
"Nelson, 62, Dies: Securities Man" (*The Chattanooga Times*, October 24, 1972), A1, 2.

Nieland-Overmyer Musical Angels Windows
Obituary of Donald Howard Overmyer (*The Chattanooga Times*, October 2, 1990), A4.

Obituary of Ruth Elberfeld Overmyer (*The Chattanooga Times*, February 11, 1994), A12.

Robert Wernick, "Brother Angel: When He Took Holy Orders He Was Fra Giovanni; In Time His Spiritual Manner and Heavenly Painting Gave Him a Truer Name, Fra Angelico," Smithsonian (December 1986), 46-57.

Noll Window
"Dedicate Window at St. Paul's: Honors Memory of Late Fred A. Noll: Impressive Ceremony Conducted by Dr. John D. Wing Yesterday Morning" (*The Chattanooga Times*, June 9, 1924), 5.
"Dedication of the Noll Memorial Window" (The Chimes, St. Paul's Episcopal Church, Chattanooga, Tenn., June 8, 1924).
"Frederick Noll Dies; Funeral Tomorrow" (*The Chattanooga Times*, October 17, 1923).
John Wilson, "Hamilton County Pioneers: The Schneiders" (The Chattanoogan, October 21, 2007).

Patten Light of the World Window
Biography of Z.C. Patten, from *History of Chattanooga, Tennessee*, 465-6.
"3 New Windows Put In" (Chattanooga News-Free Press, November 26, 1981).
"Area Philanthropist Elizabeth Patten Dies," (*The Chattanooga Times*, February 9, 1990), A-6.
"Death Comes to Z.C. Patten at 'Ashland': Leading Business Man and Pioneer Citizen: Cheerful, Patient During Last Hours" (*The Chattanooga Times*, March 21, 1925), 3.
"Elizabeth Patten Dies: Noted Preservationist," (Chattanooga News-Free Press, February 9, 1990), A-1.
"History in Glass" (*The Chattanooga Times*, December 19, 1981), F-1.
"Mrs. Patten Dies at the Age of 93: Her Family Always Part of City's History—Funeral 10:30 A.M. Saturday" (*The Chattanooga Times*, July 18, 1958), A-1.
"Mrs. Patten Dies at Age 93: Member of Old, Prominent Family" (Chattanooga News-Free Press, July 17, 1958).
"Prominent Business Leader Z. Cartter Patten Jr. Dies," (Chattanooga News-Free Press, February 5, 1982), A-1.
"Z.C.Patten Dies at Age 84 after Life of Service: End Comes after Illness of Several Weeks at Home Near Flintstone, Ga." (Chattanooga News, March 21, 1925), 3.
"Z. Cartter Patten Jr., Civic Leader, Is Dead" (*The Chattanooga Times*, February 8, 1982), 1.
Alfred Fisher, Chapel Studio, London, England, to the Stained Glass Committee of St. Paul's Episcopal Church, Chattanooga, Tenn., November 13, 1980.
Gilbert Govan, "Over My Shoulder" (*The Chattanooga Times*, March 27, 1975), A-8.
Lila McLeod, "Telling the Story in Glass: Combining History, Scenery and the Message of St. Paul's Episcopal Church Was a Challenge to London Artisans" (Chattanooga News-Free Press, November 26, 1981), I-1 with photo on A-1.
Mary M. Reynolds, "Backward-Looking and Forward-Looking at Once" (*The Chattanooga Times*, February 18, 1968).
Mary Macdonald Reynolds, "Ascertain Facts, Express Opinion, Is Patten Creed" (*The Chattanooga Times*, March 26, 1958).
John Wilson, *The Patten Chronicle: The Story of a Great Chattanooga Family* (Chattanooga, Tenn.: Roy McDonald, [1986]).

Rathburn Window
East Tennessee: Historical and Biographical (Chattanooga, Tenn.: A.D. Smith & Co., 1893), 230-2.
"Mrs. Katherine D. Rathburn: Well-Known Resident Died at Her Home Last Night" (*The Chattanooga Times*, March 21, 1910), 3.

Ray Window
Obituary of Mrs. Frances McMullan Ray (*The Chattanooga Times*, December 13, 1974), 13.
Obituary of Betty Ray (*Chattanooga Times Free Press*, October 20, 1999).
Obituary of Dr. Charles Ray (*Chattanooga Times Free Press*, April 27, 2001).

Record Window
Alfred Fisher, Chapel Studio, London, England, to Joe Duncan, Chattanooga, Tenn., April 30, 1982.
Harmon Jolley, "Have a Seat, and Read about the Milne Chair Company," Chattanoogan.com, Chattanooga, Tenn., April 28, 2010.
Obituary of Margaret Milne Record (*The Chattanooga Times*, October 1, 1983).
Dr. W.D.L. Record Dies; Former Erlanger Chief (*The Chattanooga Times*, November 12, 1983).

Reeves Windows
"Dr. James E. Reeves: Death of the Eminent Physician Yesterday Afternoon" (*The Sunday Times*, Chattanooga, Tenn., January 5, 1896), 5.
"Mrs. Frances M. Reeves: Benevolent Woman Dies at a Ripe Old Age" (*The Daily Times*, Chattanooga, Tenn., May 6, 1908).
New York State Medical Society, "Obituary of Dr. James Edmund Reeves," The Medical News 68, no. 7 (February 15, 1896), 196.
Louisiana State Medical Society, New Orleans Medical and Surgical Journal 23, no. 8 (February 1896), 501.

Staley Window
"A Beautiful Window: Erected by St. Agnes Guild in Memory of Miss Jennie Staley," transcript (The Chattanooga News, February 23, 1892), 4.
"The Deadly Pistol: Miss Jennie Staley Meets with a Serious Accident" (*The Daily Times*, Chattanooga, Tenn., March 27, 1891), 4.
"The Dreadful End: Miss Jennie Staley Finds Relief in Death Yesterday" (*The Daily Times*, Chattanooga, Tenn., March 30, 1891), 5.
Obituary of Laura Staley Voigt (*The Chattanooga Times*, May 28, 1953).
Whittington Johnson, *Black Savannah, 1788-1864* (Fayetteville, Ark.: University of Arkansas Press, 1999), 16.
Biography of Hon. Hugh Whiteside, *History of East Tennessee* (Chicago and Nashville: Goodspeed Publishing Company: 1887).

www.ingramcontent.com/pod-product-compliance
Lightning Source LLC
LaVergne TN
LVHW051039070526
838201LV00066B/4860